How Do I Look from Up There?

You, from God's point of view

Lois Dodds

VICTOR BOOKS

a division of SP Publications, Inc.

WHEATON, ILLINOIS 60187

Offices also in Fullerton, California • Whitby, Ontario, Canada • Amersham-on-the-Hill, Bucks, England

Bible quotations are from the *New American Standard Bible* (NASB), © 1960, 1962, 1963, 1968, 1971, 1972, 1973, 1975, by permission of the Lockman Foundation; *The Living Bible* (LB), Tyndale House Publishers, used by permission; the *New International Version* (NIV), © 1978 by The New York International Bible Society; *The New Testament in Modern English* (PH), © J.B. Phillips 1960, first American edition, The Macmillan Company; *The Modern Language Bible* (BERK), copyrighted by Zondervan Publishing House. Unidentified quotations are from the King James Version.

Library of Congress Catalog Card Number: 80-51160
ISBN: 0-88207-584-5

VICTOR BOOKS
A division of SP Publications, Inc.
P.O. Box 1825 ● Wheaton, Ill. 60187

How Do I Look from Up There is for you! When you know who you are to God, you'll have the key to a better self-concept.

You may use this book alone or in a group. A leader's guide with visual aids and Rip-Offs are available from your local Christian bookstore or from the publisher.

Contents

Author's Note

"You've got to love yourself!" the world says. It seems impossible to open a popular magazine without reading something about self-love, self-esteem, self-worth, self-image, or self-concept. What is all this self-talk really about? Christians especially seemed confused about it. After all, Jesus said, "Deny yourself. Take up your cross . . ." Is it right to love yourself or to think highly of yourself, or does this contradict Scripture?

This book will help you sort out the confusing, opposing ideas and will help you see yourself as *God* sees you. When you know your value to Him, your feeling of worth will grow. "As a man thinketh in his heart, so is he" (Proverbs 23:7). That's why it is crucial to think the *right* things about yourself. How you think about yourself, the way you value *you,* determines what you become. It shapes the way you feel and influences the way you behave. What you believe about yourself determines what you get done, and whether you will reach the potential God has given you.

Charlie Chaplin, it's said, could imitate the beautiful singing of Caruso. But he claimed he couldn't sing. He saw himself as a comic, so he wouldn't use his ability to sing opera. He could have been a singer, but he only saw himself as a mimic.

God's Word is your best mirror. It tells you how to value yourself. It tells you why God sees you as someone special. Get acquainted with who you really are. But first . . .

I'd like to tell you about myself, and why the things in this book are so important to me. I am the 8th in a family of 12 children. I didn't always feel loved or wanted. Life was hard and sometimes very confusing. But I made an exciting discovery:

God thinks I am somebody. As I got to know Him and His Word, I discovered that He loves me, and has something special planned for me. I found out that even though I don't often impress people, I can have a purpose in my life and use all the gifts God has given me by serving Him. I found the strength to go through tough times and the courage to accept opportunities. I grew because of God's love and the confidence He gave me. Little by little I discovered 12 fantastic reasons to think well of myself. Because of who I am in Christ, I accept myself and find much happiness in my life. By trusting Him, I've been spared many tragedies which have happened in the lives of my relatives (there've been 3 suicides and close to 30 divorces).

My husband Larry and I serve God through the Wycliffe Bible Translators. We've lived in Peru for 10 years, working with about 50 ethnic groups. We have three teenage children—David, Kathryn, and Michael—who continually help us grow and give.

I hope that these truths which protected and changed me will help you. May you see yourself as the unique and precious person God created you to be!

—Lois

Acknowledgements

I want to thank my friends who read all or parts of this book and gave me helpful suggestions: Richard Houston, Martha Weaver, Susan Schneider, Christine Wood, and Hugh Steven.

I appreciate the help of three of my best treasures —my children David, Kathryn, and Michael. They gave me helpful suggestions and, of course, years of experience with teenage minds. Kathryn typed and proofread for me, and David and Michael helped in other ways. I also appreciate the wholehearted encouragement of my husband Larry and his advice on theological matters.

My students at Yarinacocha High School in Peru allowed me to try out this material on them in class.

Dr. Wendell Searer, our friend and pediatrician, first suggested I write for teens on the topic of self-esteem. Dr. David Kirk, professor of education at Azusa Pacific College, encouraged me to do this project. I am also grateful to Charles and Rosalie Dahl for offering us a peaceful and quiet place to write—their cabin at Hume Lake.

Most of all, I want to thank my heavenly Father and my dear Saviour and friend Jesus for lovingly teaching me and for giving me this opportunity to share with you.

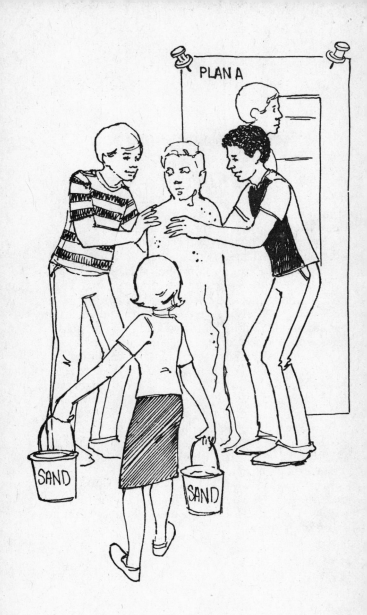

1

You're More than You Think!

Imagine that you're in Israel, standing on Mt. Tabor, when you see a magnificent church. Your curiosity gets the best of you, so you venture inside and sit in a back pew. As you watch, you see a lovely transformation taking place on the front wall. The setting sun's rays shine into the church through a high window at the entrance and creep toward a mosaic of Christ on the wall, gradually transforming it into a radiant glowing figure. You can't make out any details of the figure—all you can see is the golden aura of the sun shining on Christ.

When you allow Christ to reflect His love through you, your life is transformed in much the same way as this mosaic is transformed by the sunlight. He shines on every area of your life, until other people see Him through you.

If you visit the Steuben crystal factory, you can crowd in along the rail that separates the tourists from the glassmakers and watch the artisans as they take the red-hot liquid glass from huge brick furnaces and shape it skillfully into glasses, vases, or figures.

Some pieces of glass art made by Steuben sell for as much as $25,000! Only a few pieces of certain items are made. This enhances their value; people pay incredible prices for these rare pieces because they are not common reproductions.

You'd expect something that expensive to be composed mainly of rare elements, but it's not so.

Steuben glass is 40% lead! You know what that's like. Perhaps you've used a piece on your fishing line. Lead is dull and gray and heavy. It's definitely not transparent. There's no way you can see through it; it's as opaque as any element can be.

The crystal also contains silica, the common sand you've seen in a sandbox or on the beach. Lead and sand. With the addition of some chemicals, the glass recipe is complete.

Try mixing some lead, some sand, and some chemicals. It's a strange mixture—nothing like the crystal goblet on your mom's table. What else is needed?

Glassmakers know that to turn those ingredients into crystal, they must use a special process—*heat*. The crystal is heated *hotter than liquid steel* (about 350° F). When it is molten it can be shaped and cut. As it cools it becomes transparent and brilliant.

You're like that Steuben crystal! You're made of common elements (the Genesis account says "dust"), but you are put together in an awesome way by the world's greatest Artist. He shaped you and breathed His own breath into you. You're unique because He formed you individually; you weren't poured into a mold. So you're valuable and special.

Worth $5,554,000?

Did you ever wonder why someone would pay $5,554,000 for a painting, as someone did for the "Portrait of Juan De Pareja" by Velasquez?

The value of art is determined by the *quality* of the work, by *who the artist is*, and by what the art "*says*." Some works of high quality are done on ordinary materials, but that doesn't lessen their worth. Michelangelo's frescoes on the ceiling of the Sistine chapel, for example, are priceless—but they're painted on plaster. Their quality, the fact that Michelangelo painted them, and their profound message make them great.

You are valuable for the same reasons. The most fantastic Artist of all time—God Himself—made you. You're greater than any art or machine man has made.

Can you see yourself as wonderfully made? As made by the same God who made all the beauty of the world and the universe?

Know God—Know Yourself

The best way to know who you really are is to know who God is. The Bible, of course, is a Book about God, about His Son Jesus, and about His relationships with people.

One of the most revealing things the Bible shows about God is that He is *always* involved with people. The first chapter, Genesis 1, tells how God created the universe including people. The last chapter in the Book of Revelation records God's future fellowship with man. Every chapter in between is also about God relating to people. This shows that *God cares deeply*

about us—each of us. We are tremendously important to Him.

Check out King David's meditations about how
man fits into God's universe:

> When I consider Your heavens,
>   the work of Your fingers,
> the moon and the stars,
>   which You have set in place,
> what is man that You are mindful of him,
>   the son of man that You care for him?
> You made him a little lower than the
>   heavenly beings
> and crowned him with glory and honor.
>
> You made him ruler over the works of
>   Your hands;
> You put everything under his feet
> (Psalm 8:3-6, NIV).

"God Don't Make Junk!"

Yes, God made you, and every other person, for a
special purpose. He created you because of His *love*,
so you could be His child and friend. He made you to
show the rest of creation what He is like.

Of course, many people don't believe God made
them or that they have a purpose. They choose to
believe they're still just dust—dirt cheap and ex-
pendable. Some believe they're no more than animals; modern "behaviorists" see people as bio-
chemical machines that can be programmed or
coded genetically. Existentialists say people's lives
have no meaning, except for what they can make for
themselves.

If you know God's point of view, you can toss these philosophies. You can see yourself as God sees you. A poster that hung in a converted drug addict's room in a rehabilitation center said, "God made me—and God don't make junk!"

People who don't know God don't know the basis of their worth. They think their value depends on their
> beauty
>> wealth
>>> intelligence
>>>> status
>>>>> job
>>>>>> power
>>>>>>> personality.

But this is not what God says!

Yes, But . . .

One of the biggest hang-ups people have in believing that God made mankind is that humans have so many problems. It's true—nobody's perfect. People have *big* problems—like selfishness, greed, pride. You and everybody else are weak and fragile, and won't last too long on earth. You've all fallen short of what God had in mind for you.

But none of these things makes you worthless in God's eyes. The Bible shows why you aren't exactly as He planned you. The Bible also points the way toward God's plan to eventually make you perfect.

When Adam and Eve sinned, God didn't scratch humans from His *To Be Loved* list. Instead, He began immediately to provide a way to make people right again.

But I Can't Keep from Sinning!

God made you in His image, as He made Adam and Eve back in the Garden of Eden. You probably know the story of how they sinned and how their sin affected us all. (We'll talk more about this in chapter 5.)

Through Adam, sin became part of us. We can't escape sin and death even if we refuse to recognize them. We all have the capacity to do evil; none of us ever chooses to always do what's right (Romans 3:23).

God made us to know and do good. It was Satan's idea for us to also know evil. Because of sin we often choose to go *our* way instead of God's. But because God loves us, He gives us a second chance—through Jesus.

"But God demonstrates His own love toward us, in that while we were yet sinners, Christ died for us" (Romans 5:8, NASB).

Sin does not have to be a permanent part of you, to destroy God's purposes for you. Jesus is the remedy!

Here Today, Gone Tomorrow

None of us will last long, compared with the wide scope of time. This shakes up some people. It hurts their pride. So they think life doesn't really matter.

Bildad the Shuhite, the unfriendly friend of Job in the Old Testament, argued this point often. "Man is just a blade of grass," he said. "You're just a worm, Job. Why don't you give up and die?"

But Job knew God better than Bildad and his other buddies did. Job said, "Though [God] slay me, yet will I trust in Him" (Job 13:15). Job knew life on earth was only a fraction of his total existence. To die, even at God's hand, meant he would be with God forever.

The fact that you won't be staying long on earth in no way makes you worthless. Some of the most costly, beautiful, and useful things in life don't last too long, but they make a huge difference. A glorious sunset changes fast; a powerful lightning flash singes the sky in an instant; a smile takes only a moment— but each is loaded with meaning. And so are you.

But I'm So Weak

The Apostle Paul wrote, "When I am weak, then I am strong" (2 Corinthians 12:10). He knew what many psychologists have only recently learned: A person can't be strong without having come to grips with his weakness.

You too are weak because of sin. There's always a war going on in you—and sin wins unless you have God's Holy Spirit to crush it.

But just because you're weak doesn't mean you are worthless. Learning how to handle your weakness is the important thing. Paul could say, "When I am weak, then I am strong," because he knew that *in his weakness he needed to live on God's power instead of his own.* You can learn to do that too.

God loves the weak and humble. But He's not wild about the haughty who don't think they need Him.

For thus says the high and exalted One
Who lives forever, whose name is Holy,
"I dwell on a high and holy place,
And also with the contrite and lowly of spirit
In order to revive the spirit of the lowly

And to revive the heart of the contrite. . . .
I have seen his ways, but I will heal him;
I will lead him and restore comfort to him"
(Isaiah 57:15, 18, NASB).

How Do You Look to You?

Most parents, teachers, and psychologists agree that
it's healthy to have a good self-image—to feel good
about yourself and to believe you are worth something.

But even though it's healthy to like yourself, most
people don't—and this leads to all kinds of trouble. If
you don't like *you*, it's hard to be your best self and to
like other people.

Since you are made in God's image, why do you
often feel so bad about yourself? (If you're one of the
few who feels good about himself, rejoice! You're an
exceptional person!) Let's look at some reasons.

Where Does Your Self-Image Come From?

You have a certain picture of yourself—of your face,
your body, your personality, your mind, your spirit.
Stop a minute and review this mental image. Are you
tall? Short? Spirited? Depressed? Excitable and
interesting, or dull and boring? Think about this
picture. Where did you get it? Is it 100% accurate?

Most of what you know about yourself you
learned from other people. When you were a baby,
you began drawing your mental self-image by the
way people responded to you. If they fed you
cheerfully when you cried, burped you when you

had a bubble, changed your diapers on time, and hugged and kissed you often, you probably began to form a good picture of yourself. But if people neglected you, and were angry around you, you probably formed a negative image of yourself.

Tragically, some people have such grim lives as infants and children that they learn to hate themselves and everyone else.

While the early years seem to be the most crucial in shaping your self-image, you keep on forming it all through life. Everyone around you—your parents, brothers, sisters, friends, the man at the gas pump— acts as a mirror to help you see yourself. People send you either positive messages that make you feel good about yourself, or negative ones that make you feel bad.

Just as you don't accurately reflect God's image because of the effects of Adam's and Eve's sins, not everyone reflects you fairly. For instance, if you innocently ask for a cookie and your mother screams at you, you probably get the message, "You're bad— don't bother me!" But the truth may be that she has a terrible headache and would scream at anyone. And of course, you get other unfavorable reflections of yourself because you do some things that really aren't OK.

OK—or Not OK?

This mix-up in messages makes it difficult to form a true picture of yourself. Thomas Harris, in his book *I'm OK—You're OK*, says that it's the *dependency* we all have to live through that makes us feel "not OK." Because we all start out as babies, totally helpless and at the mercy of other people, he says we all feel "not OK" to start with. We have to learn later how to feel "OK" about ourselves.

But there's something more. Harris' theory doesn't include a way to handle our true moral guilt. We're all sinful, and we all feel "not OK." These two are related.

God made you for Himself but sin interferes with your knowing and loving Him so you can't feel OK about yourself. Only if your sin is taken care of and you get to know God can you be "OK." An airplane can't run on diesel if it is designed for aviation gas. And you can't feel OK if you have only people-power and no God-power in your life.

How Can You Change Your Self-Image?

Did you ever prowl around your Grandma's attic when you were younger? You probably saw a lot of old stuff up there—chairs, clothes, trunks, maybe old books, or even her love letters. What you thought was just junk might actually have been expensive antiques. If you've read any books lately about the value of old furniture, you probably wish you hadn't been so rough on that old rocker or the cradle that your great grandfather made. Learning from the experts has increased your appreciation of that "junk."

The key to changing your self-image is in knowing what God, the People Expert, says about you.

Here are three things you can do to see yourself the right way and to help you feel good about yourself:

1. **Look at what God says about you.** That's what this book is for.

2. **Accept what God says about you.** That means

admitting God made you, and that even though you are sinful, He wants to restore you so you can know Him.

3. **Act out God's values.** That will give you good messages about you from other people. They will be able to see God in you. And you will start to feel better about yourself because of God's approval and people's appreciation.

You Are Special Because . . .

Every person who has ever lived has four things in common with you—four reasons why he and you are special:

1. You are made by God.
2. You are made in God's image—patterned after Him.
3. You are made to do good.
4. Your sin was paid for by Jesus, God's Son. He died for everyone, but not everyone accepts Him or His death. *If* you believe He has paid for *your* sin and made *you* His child, there are even more reasons why you are special:
5. You are chosen by God.
6. You are God's home. He lives in *you*.
7. You are an heir of God—you will inherit part of what He gives to Jesus.
8. You are a priest of God.
9. You share Jesus' life and His future.
10. You give joy and friendship to God.
11. You are a gift of God and for God.
12. You are a becomer!

Impressed? Keep reading!

2

You're a Designer Original

My sister Becky is a designer. She's designed many "Hang Ten," "Catalina," and "Jantzen" sports clothes. You don't see her name in them, but ideas for shirts and other items come off her drawing board. They carry the label of the company she works for. These labels become the manufacturers' trademarks, and serve as a guarantee of quality.

God has labeled you in many ways too. Instead of Hang Ten's little footprints on your chest, He has left His imprint on you in other ways. He's put a thousand clues in your heart, mind, and body to help you find out where you came from.

God, the Master Designer

God is the Creator of all things. Genesis (chapters 1 and 2) gives us the first outline of what God made.

Other writers in the Bible also speak of God as the Creator of everything. In one of my favorite Psalms, 104, David praises God for His works. He sums them up, saying: "O Lord, what a variety You have made! And in wisdom You have made them all! The earth is full of Your riches" (Psalm 104:24, LB).

As God told Isaiah:

> It is I who made the earth, and created man upon it. I stretched out the heavens with My hands, and I ordained all their host (Isaiah 45:12, NASB).

Isaiah repeats God's words, and emphasizes that God made the world to be *inhabited*.

> For Jehovah created the heavens and the earth and put everything in place, and He made the world to be lived in, not to be an empty chaos (45:18, LB).

God's Specialty: Man

If we look carefully at the first account of Creation in Genesis, we see that God made man differently from the way He made the universe, the plants, and the animals.

Look through chapter 1. Notice how many times God says, "Let there be . . ." He does this all the way through Creation into the sixth day, when He makes man. "Let there be . . ." is a rather impersonal and *passive* way for God to talk. We know of course that God is using His power, and that His word alone is strong enough to bring into being all the things He creates, but the passive command doesn't show *how* He is involved.

Do you see the dramatic contrast in the sixth day? It's as though God suddenly shifts into high gear, and talks to Himself instead of to the universe:

"Let Us make man in Our image" He says. "*Let Us make.*" This command is *active*. God gets *personally* involved in making man. He doesn't get as involved when He makes the stars or the oceans or the plants. But He creates man in *His own image!*

"Mouth-to-Mouth" Resuscitation

There's a "flashback" in Genesis that shows us more about how God made man:

> Then the Lord God formed man of dust from the ground, and breathed into his nostrils the breath of life; and man became a living being (Genesis 2:7, NASB).

Look how intimately God is involved in making man! *He breathes into him with His own breath.* That's pretty intimate. Not long ago I breathed life back into a baby dying of whooping cough—an awesome experience. My husband, a doctor, has done that often to save someone's life. But how much more special it is when we see *God* breathing into man in the beginning, to make him come alive— giving man His own breath, His own Spirit!

Caution: Potter at Work

When I think of God making us from dust, I think of making pottery. Isaiah, the prophet, uses this comparison to describe how God personally made us:

"And yet, O Lord, You are our Father. We are the clay and You are the Potter. We are all formed by Your hand" (Isaiah 64:8, LB).

Since I've lived in South America, my understanding of pottery has increased, because it's so much a part of life for many Indian groups. The potter spends much time and effort in making his pottery. He gathers sticky clay from a riverbank or other muddy place. He stores it carefully to keep it damp and pliable. He shapes the pieces carefully, squatting for hours in an uncomfortable position. Unless he uses a potter's wheel, each piece has its own identity. In Peru, for example, each tribe has its distinctive shapes and designs and each potter has his own style.

Making pottery takes dedication. A potter has to wait for days for his pots to dry. Then he gathers just the right firewood and cuts it to the right size to bake his pots. Since many potters use an open fire, rather than a kiln, it takes special skill to know when to clear the fire away.

This truth about how God personally made us is repeated in other ways in the Bible. In a beautiful poem, David says:

You made all the delicate, inner parts of my body, and knit them together in my mother's womb. Thank You for making me so wonderfully complex! It is amazing to think about. Your workmanship is marvelous—and how well I know it. . . . You saw me before I was born and scheduled each day of my life before I began to breathe. Every day was recorded in Your Book.

How precious it is, Lord, to realize that You are thinking about me constantly! I can't even count how many times a day Your thoughts turn towards me. And when I waken in the morning, You are still thinking of me! (Psalm 139:13-18, LB)

People with a Purpose

Again in the New Testament, Paul describes God's handiwork in mankind. He tells the men of Athens, who are ignorant of God:

> He made the world and everything in it, and since He is Lord of heaven and earth, He doesn't live in man-made temples. . . . He Himself gives life and breath to everything, and satisfies every need there is. He created all the people of the world from one man, Adam, and scattered the nations across the face of the earth. . . . His purpose in all this is that they should seek after God, and perhaps feel their way toward Him and find Him—though He is not far from any one of us. For in Him we live and move and are! (Acts 17:24-28a, LB)

Not only did God make you, but He made you *with a purpose.* He wasn't acting out some fantasy when He created the universe. He had a purpose for making everything—including you.

Destined to Be Born

God's intention even before He created the world was to make people in order that He might adopt them to be His sons. He did this out of one purpose: *love!* God wanted to have children and friends—people He could love and who would love Him.

That is why He made *you!* (Ephesians 1:4-5)

You probably know the famous "all things work together for good" verse in Romans 8. God has called us *"according to His purpose"* (8:28). Yes, God has a purpose for you! "For we are God's workmanship, created in Christ Jesus to do good works, which God prepared in advance for us to do" (Ephesians 2:10, NIV).

Copyright—by God

When you think about yourself, remember this: *God made you.* He planned long before He made the world that you would be born, in order that you might have the opportunity to become His child. He has a wonderful design for you and your life. He wants you to discover Him and His plan. As you get to know Him, you'll become more like the person God had in mind all along. As you reflect Him, you will be "filled full" with satisfaction and pleasure.

The View from Down Here

1. How has God left His "imprint" on your character?

2. Why do you suppose God wanted to get personally involved in making humans?

3. Can you see traits in your personality that show you're made in God's image?

4. How can you bring out more of the Godlike qualities in your life? How can you discover and develop other qualities that you're not even aware of?

5. Since God made you to be unique, can you think of ways in which you're different from everyone else?

3

God's Reflection in You

"Hey, he looks just like you!" some people would tell me when they saw our young son David. But then someone else would say, "He looks just like his dad!" That confused me. How could he look just like me and just like my husband Larry too?

Then one day Larry was working in our darkroom, printing pictures we'd taken of each other. He decided to print a picture with half of my face and half his. But, instead of getting some funny face, he came from the darkroom amazed. Our faces almost matched. We had a good laugh. David can't disown us. It is too obvious that we are his parents.

Your Heavenly I.D.

Your physical characteristics are clues that tell people who your parents are. Many of your personal

31

qualities are signs of your heavenly identity too. God made you in His own image, in His own likeness. This means you are a complex person. You can think, as God does. You have feelings, as He does. You can make moral choices. You are a spirit, as He is— you're more than just a body.

You Look like God

After God created the universe, He turned His attention to making man. He said:

> "Let Us make man in Our image, according to Our likeness. . . ." And God created man in His own image, in the image of God He created him; male and female He created them (Genesis 1:26-27, NASB).

God personally formed man and breathed His own life into him. But God wasn't finished yet. He said, "It is not good for the man to be alone; I will make him a helper suitable for him" (2:18, NASB).

God made man and woman to go together, but He created the two individually. God formed Adam from the dust, but when He was ready to make Eve, He chose to make her out of a part of Adam's rib. (See Genesis 2:21-24.)

While we don't know all about how maleness and femaleness apply to God, He implies that these sexual distinctions somehow reflect part of His own image. God thought it was good to make both man and woman. The two are equal in His mind.

Some psychologists say that every person has both masculine and feminine characteristics, and that balance in one's personality depends on learning to harness these and use them wisely. But this balance is sometimes hard to achieve, especially when everything around us tells us something different.

As a young person, I was afraid to seem too logical, because it wasn't considered feminine. "Smart girls never let a man know how smart they are," people said.

This problem doesn't affect only girls. I know a guy who roars around on his motorcycle and talks tough. Under that macho exterior, he really cares for people. But he's afraid it isn't masculine to be loving and gentle.

Scripture is full of illustrations which show that God has both of what our culture calls "masculine" and "feminine" characteristics. For instance, Jesus had compassion on the blind man and gave him back his sight (Mark 8:23-24). But He's also the mighty Protector who sends His angels to protect His children, as He did for Daniel in the lions' den (Daniel 6:17-22) and for the Israelites on many occasions (Isaiah 43:1-3).

You are either male or female by God's design, and both are good. Both serve God's purpose and reflect His qualities.

What's in a Name?

Let's back up a little. Before we can fully know what it means to be created in God's image, we have to understand who God is.

Remember the story of Moses at the burning bush? (Exodus 3) Moses wanted to know how to answer the grumbling Israelite elders when they asked who sent him. God said, "Tell them I AM WHO I AM."

God could have used something really mind-boggling, such as "I am the greatest!" or "I am the Person who can either squash you or make you king over the entire world!"

But He didn't. He said simply, "I AM." He put the focus on His existence as a Person.

Notice that God didn't come out and say, "I am the Person who created the world," or "I am the One who can *do* anything." He didn't call Himself "I DO."

In most of the world, a person's value is determined by what he does, rather than by what he is—a living, breathing person. The Western world is usually preoccupied with the battle to "get ahead," to get a good education, to have money, to enjoy "the good life." We have the wrong values about what makes people worthwhile. If we don't see people as "useful," it is easy to think they aren't important, that they are worth less than "useful" people. We are seldom content to value people just because they're God's creations.

Though most people judge your worth by what you do or what you own, God loves you just because you're you. His love for you doesn't depend on your ability to achieve, your beauty, your intelligence, and all the other qualities people use to judge you. It's as though God says, "I love you because I made you—you are Mine."

You are a "human being," not a "human doing." What you *are* in God's eyes is more important than what you are able to *do*. Suppose you blow an algebra test, or you're not invited to your best friend's party, or you realize you'll never get higher than the third-string water boy on your football team. Are you worthless? Or are you still great in God's eyes?

You can base your worth on the fact that God

made you one of His creations. When you under-stand who He says you are, you'll be able to do things that please Him. Even if you think your life is shat-tered when something bad happens, God still loves you.

The neat thing about this is that when you accept the fact that God made you a unique person, you have the courage to be yourself. You don't have to act like someone else, or pretend to be what you are not.

You Can Think!

God didn't program you to be a robot or a computer. He created you with a mind, with curiosity, with a desire for knowledge. He gave you the capacity to make decisions. He gave you the ability to be like Him by searching, musing, planning, and evaluating —you are even free to believe He doesn't exist and that He didn't make you!

God made you capable of making moral choices. He gave Adam and Eve this ability too. They knew right away when they had sinned. No one had to tell them. They hid from God because they felt guilty. After they sinned, God said, "Behold, the man has become like one of Us, knowing good and evil" (Genesis 3:22, NASB).

God trusted man enough to give him intelligence. Do you think the current "knowledge explosion" is a surprise to God? He must have fun watching people discover His creation bit by bit. Maybe He watches excitedly when a scientist is discovering something wonderful, or when an artist makes an original design. "In [Christ] are hidden all the treasures of wisdom and knowledge" (Colossians 2:3, NASB).

You Have Feelings

You have feelings; so does God. His are reflected in
you. Most of us know that He's joyful and tender
(Psalm 25:6-7). He is loving (1 John 4:8). But He also
gets angry sometimes (Deuteronomy 1:34). He
grieves (John 11:30-36). He is delighted (Isaiah 62:4).
He expresses His emotions, and He chose to make us
emotional too.

When I was young, I didn't understand anything
about God's emotions except that some people said
He was angry most of the time. Somehow I
concluded that to feel any kind of emotion was
sinful, so I tried to never let mine show. I tried to
never let anyone see me cry, and I bit my tongue if I
was angry. I never let myself giggle or laugh. As a
teenager and an adult, I have had an exciting time
discovering that I don't have to hide my emotions. I
can let them help make my life rich.*

You Have a Spirit

God is also a Spirit; He made you with a spirit too.

The mass media emphasizes people's physical
beings. The porno industry, sex films, and certain
TV shows thrive because many people think that
only bodies are important. Whatever looks good and
feels good often becomes the standard.

This attitude, unfortunately, often goes unchal-
lenged. One day I went to my son's elementary
school to talk with the school psychologist about a

---

*For a good description of some of God's emotions, see "God Has Feelings Too," in
Caution: Christians under Construction by Bill Hybels, Victor Books, 1978.
It's another SONPOWER elective.

special program my son was in. As I sat down in his office, I noticed a poster of a beautiful forest scene with a cute chipmunk climbing a tree. The bold print said, "If it feels good, do it." That disturbed me.

"Haven't you thought of the implications of that?" I asked the psychologist, pointing to the poster.

"No. Why should I?" he said.

"Well, it seems that one responsibility of schools is to train children not to do something just because it feels good. Would you let the class bully smash someone in the face because it felt good to him? It certainly wouldn't feel good to the other child!"

"Oh," he said thoughtfully. He said he'd take the poster down or change the caption. I hope he did, because that philosophy is deadly.

Take Christi, for example. Her story is one example of what happens when people are seen as only physical bodies. She's five-feet-seven and slender. Her brown hair and blue eyes are perfect for her peachy complexion. She started dating a macho-type guy, who little by little talked her into thinking that only her body mattered, until she often gave it away. Too late she found herself alone, rejected, with the real, inner Christi starved by misuse.

Anna's story is different because she recognizes how important her inner spirit is. She has a fragile beauty, a delicate look, and a gentle spirit. She had always wanted to be loved and wanted. A married man she worked with adored her. She loved him too because he was a fine man and made her feel important. But she recognized the danger. She knew that what she did with that love was crucial and would have results through all her life. With God's strength she kept clear of sex, though she struggled hard with temptation. She didn't endanger her future for something that might have felt good at the time.

God wants you to take good care of your spirit. It's the most beautiful and enduring part of you. He doesn't want you to abuse it.

How can you move toward being the full and open spirit God wants you to be? How can you nourish your spirit? You have gym at school to exercise your body. Have you thought about spiritual exercises to stretch your spirit and help it grow? Try making a habit of reading your Bible for 15 minutes each morning. Then think of someone you know who really needs help, and pray for that person. You'll soon start feeling great about your exercises—even better than you do after 20 minutes of running.

Don't feed your spirit junk food. Nourish it with great books, wise relationships, and time with God!

You Have a Personality

Did you ever think about what makes you an individual?

God is the Creator of your individuality. He made you with a personality all your own. Though you share many traits with your family, and some with your friends, you are still a unique person. So am I. This fact encourages me to be myself, since I am the only person in the whole world who can reflect God with the particular personality that I have. It is only in knowing God that we become truly ourselves (Colossians 2:10).

You Are Creative

If you took all the great inventors, artists, musicians, and architects who have ever lived, and rolled them into one person, you still couldn't match God as a Creator. He made the whole universe. Even His microscopic creations have intricate designs. No one can even come close to organizing things the way He does. Yet God has shared His ability to plan, design, and create with humans.

Because you are made in God's image, you are a creator too. You get the urge to make things—to build or bake or paint. Maybe you like to write poems or express ideas in song. Perhaps you like to design your own clothes or plant seeds to watch them grow. All of these abilities point straight back to God as your Creator.

Your creativity is not restricted to "artistic" things. You can be original in developing relationships and inventive in solving problems. When you enjoy the freedom that comes from having a close relationship with God, your creativity can blossom because you are at ease with who you are. In Him you can become your most expressive self.

Made for Love

One of the first things God said after He created man was that he shouldn't be alone—he shouldn't be without love (Genesis 2:18). So He created woman.

But love between man and woman wasn't the only kind of love God wished for people. When asked what the greatest commandment was, Jesus said there were two:

"You shall love the Lord your God will all your heart, and with all your soul, and with all your mind." This is the great and foremost commandment. The second is like it, "You shall love your neighbor as yourself" (Matthew 22:37-39, NASB).

God revealed Himself to us as a Person who values communication and love. He wants us to love Him first, and then love others with the love He gives us.

My being loved depends on my willingness and openness to share what I am. My sharing produces a sense of trust and closeness which makes people want to love me.

Love demands communication and expression. If you love someone but get no attention in return, your love will probably wither away. That's the difference between God's love and ours: His love never changes.

Loving God is the most important thing you can do. But He also wants you to love your neighbor. He wants you to reach out to others as He does.

For the last few years, I've lived in Peru, where there are many cultures and languages. This makes loving more difficult because I sometimes lack the words or the understanding to express love.

One day a girl named Olga, who used to help me in the house, asked me for help. Though I admired and appreciated her, I couldn't express my love by helping her get an abortion as she requested. I tried to explain to her about God's love and His values about life, but I felt inadequate. She wouldn't change her mind. I had to wait it out while she suffered the dangerous treatments of a witch doctor.

This experience with Olga made me sad because I saw how limited I was in showing people that I loved them. I felt a great need to be alone with God. For about six weeks I spent many hours each day reading the New Testament. I began to see that His whole message to us is about *relationships*—with Him and with people. What counts to Him is our willingness to love, to help others, and to be open. Love doesn't necessarily mean giving the other person everything he wants. It means doing what is best for him.

You—the Mirror of God

Jesus was the perfect visible expression of the invisible God. He came into the world as a man to make peace, to provide a way for people to know and fellowship with God. He did that through His death, which paid for sin. (See Colossians 1:15-20.)

To those of us who receive Jesus' gift of forgiveness and salvation, God offers an incredible privilege: to become peacemakers—expressions of God's life and love here on earth. We won't be "perfect expressions," as Jesus was, but God will shine through us more and more as we allow Him to refine and purify us. (See 1 John 2:29—3:3.)

I love to go to the Indian markets in Peru where the people sell all kinds of handcraft. Last year I bought a beautiful embroidered dress. A few weeks later, a friend pointed out that my dress had never been finished! I'd been so caught up with the beauty of the needlework, I had failed to see it was incomplete.

In our appreciation for ourselves and for each other, we need to understand that we too are incomplete. God isn't finished with us yet. Though we already reflect Him in some ways, He is still polishing us, if we are Christians, so we will become better mirrors of Him.

But all of us who are Christians have no veils on our faces, but reflect like mirrors the glory of the Lord. We are transfigured in ever-increasing splendor into His own image, and the transformation comes from the Lord who is the Spirit (2 Corinthians 3:18, PH).

God is still transforming you. Your life is a growth process. God wants you to become more like Jesus was when He was here on earth: God's reflection, the perfect image of His Person.

The View from Down Here

1. Why do you think God created both man and woman? Why didn't he create just one sex?

2. As a male or female, how do you reflect characteristics of God, based on our culture's ideas of male and female characteristics? Do you think God assigns girls female characteristics and guys male characteristics as our society does?

3. How is the way God values people different from the way our society values people?

4. How did God intend for us to use the Godlike qualities He gave us (creativity, feelings, intelligence, etc.)?

4

You Are Made for Goodness' Sake

Have you ever wondered why God decided to share his love with people, instead of some other creature?

Philosophers often ask, "Why is man?" People want to know if their presence on earth has a purpose. Unfortunately, some people believe humans are a random happening, without purpose or plan. But God tells them clearly why He created them.

You need to know God's plan because His purpose can give meaning and richness to your life.

A Loving Purpose

God's purpose for you began with His love for you.

Before the foundation of the world He chose us to become, in Christ, His holy and blameless children living within His constant care. He planned, in His purpose of love, that we should be adopted as His own children through Jesus Christ (Ephesians 1:5, PH).

God didn't make you just because He liked to tinker with His creation. He planned to make you His child because of His love (1 Thessalonians 1:4).

Exhibit A

God wants you to be "Exhibit A" of His own character. The longer you know Him and live with Him, the more you become like Him.

I see how this works in my own family. My father-in-law Archie has great curiosity. He speaks with authority on many subjects. He has a great sense of humor, and he loves to teach. I see Archie's qualities and his pattern of living and thinking reproduced in Larry. Anyone who knows one knows a lot about the other. But it doesn't stop there. Our son Michael shows these same qualities, even though he's only 13. The family resemblance is unmistakable.

God wants you to become a mirror of Him. Since He is invisible, He wants to make Himself visible through you as He did through Jesus. He wants the rest of creation to find out more about Him through you.

Stop! Think about this for a minute. *What is the world finding out about God through you?* He wants you to live as a "child of the light."

As we obey the commandment to love one

another, the darkness in our lives disappears and the new light of life in Christ shines in (1 John 2:8, LB).

This idea reminds me of camping out. Did you ever take a flashlight and shine it into the bottom of your duffle bag? What happens to the darkness when the light enters? Right—it disappears. In the same way, God wants your life, as a reflection of the light of Jesus, to shine into other lives and hearts to cause their darkness to disappear.

You can do this in many ways—at school, at home, with your friends. You can be a friend to that guy or gal who's really lonely and lives on the fringe of things. You can have the courage to say "No" to drugs and sex and gossip. You can give others the courage to say "No" because *you* do. You can be so friendly and loving that people will want to know what makes you tick.

The Family Business: Reproducing God's Work

Besides revealing God's character through your personality and attitudes, you can show the world what God is like by loving and helping people, by being responsible so people can see God in you.

Jesus came into the world to make peace between God and man. He did this by paying for man's sins. We are called to be peacemakers too. Of course, we don't pay for others' sins as Jesus did, but by living out God's message of love and forgiveness, we help to make peace between them and God.

For [Christ] gave Himself for us, that He might

rescue us from all our evil ways and make for Himself a people of His own, clean and pure, with our hearts set upon living a life that is good (Titus 2:14, PH).

God promises to make you a successful peacemaker when you believe in Him. He wants you to ask Him for good fruit such as love, peace, and patience, so you can love and help other people. This will cause some of them to know God too. (See Galatians 5:22.)

Good + Good = Great!

God planned from the beginning that you should spend your life in helping others. (See Ephesians 2:10.) His Word is full of instructions about how to express love and concern for other people—to do good deeds that build up others and help them to grow. (For examples, see Colossians 3:12-16.) This is a fantastic concept: The more good you do for others, the more you grow, and the closer you get to the potential God has given you. How does this work?

When you do something good, you feel good about yourself because you are being obedient to God and living up to your own ideals. You also have the opportunity to receive good responses from other people. "Your own soul is nourished when you are kind; it is destroyed when you are cruel" (Proverbs 11:17, LB). So your doing good has double results—it's good for you and good for someone else. More importantly, it helps you to know God better. He is happy when you choose to do what He delights in (Isaiah 56:4-5).

Doing evil, in contrast, produces bad results in your life. You know how that is. When you fail to do right, or when you do wrong, you suffer by feeling guilty and having your communication with God interrupted. You also give negative impressions to other people and get negative feedback from them.

But why do you do evil things if you are made for good? Because of sin. Our sin separates us from God, and interferes with our fellowship with Him.

> Listen now! The Lord isn't too weak to save you. And He isn't getting deaf! He can hear when you call! But the trouble is that your sins have cut you off from God. Because of sin He has turned His face away from you and will not listen anymore (Isaiah 59:1-2, LB).

Sin ruins people's relationships with other people as well as with God. Even those who don't believe in God suffer the consequences of doing wrong. When Larry works as an emergency room doctor, he sees patient after patient who is there because of sin: a drunk half frozen from lying in the snow, a wife who tried to commit suicide to get back at her unloving husband, a drug addict who overdosed, a dead family who was killed by a selfish driver. It is sad how people die and suffer because God's laws are broken. Here's what the Apostle John says about it:

> Never give your hearts to this world or to any of the things in it. A man cannot love the Father and love the world at the same time. For the whole world system, based as it is on men's primitive desires, their greedy ambitions, and the glamor of all that they think splendid, is not derived from the Father at all, but from the world itself. The

world and all its passionate desires will one day disappear. But the man who is following God's will is part of the permanent and cannot die (1 John 2:15-17, PH).

Three Results of Doing Good

Knowing you're made for good affects your life in three ways. It influences what you *become;* it helps you decide how to *act;* and it changes your *life goals* and career choices. Let's take a look at how this works.

1. *Becoming.* Pascal, famous French mathematician and philosopher, said that every person has a "God-shaped vacuum" in his life. When we reach out to know God and to do what He asks of us, we fill that vacuum. He is pleased when we do things His way.

Knowing you are made for good helps you see yourself in a realistic way. You understand your potential. You have a standard for yourself; you're headed somewhere. You don't have to "let the world squeeze you into its own mold." You can "let God remold your minds from within, so that you may prove in practice that the plan of God for you is good, meets all His demands, and moves toward the goal of true maturity. . . . Don't cherish exaggerated ideas of yourself or your importance, but try to have a sane estimate of your capabilities by the light of the faith that God has given to you all" (Romans 12:2-3, PH).

Having a sane idea of your abilities means you recognize God can give you power to do good. When He does you won't brag about it. Rather you'll see how great your potential is because of God's power in you. You'll be able to give the credit to Him.

2. *Deciding How to Act.* Knowing what God wants you to become helps you in your day-to-day choices too.

Dr. Kenneth Pike is a leading linguist who has studied hundreds of the cultures and languages of the world. He says that people in every culture are "wistful to be good"—even those who practice such evils as killing babies, cannibalism, and having sex with someone else's wife. He says every culture has *some* moral standard, even though it may be far below our Christian one, and that people want to be able to fulfill the ideal.

Of course, since we have the Bible and can know what God wants for us, we have a higher standard for our moral choices. We have the Ten Commandments and hundreds of New Testament instructions from God. But when we have God's Spirit living inside us, we not only have the *desire* to do good, but also the *power* to do it (Philippians 2:13).

3. *Choosing a Career.* Knowing that God has made you for good can help you decide what to do with your life. God asks, "Why spend . . . your labor on what does not satisfy?" (Isaiah 55:2, NIV) Satisfaction means using your work and your time to do God's will—especially in helping other people to know Him.

Whenever we spend a dollar for something, we're in a sense *voting* for the product or service. By buying a certain thing, we are asking for it to be continued. This is true of the way we spend our lives too. How do you want to vote with *your* time? For God's good?

Dr. Paul Tournier, a counselor and psychiatrist, says that "the calling makes the man." He's learned that a job or a career helps to determine what a man becomes. It influences what he thinks and does.

The Apostle Paul knew this 2,000 years ago: "I . . . entreat you to walk in a manner worthy of the calling with which you have been called, with all humility and gentleness, with patience, showing forbearance to one another in love" (Ephesians 4:1, NASB).

Stop a minute. Think. What have you thought about choosing a job or a career? Look ahead. What will that work cause you to become?

When you know that God has made you for good, and has promised to help you practice it, you are miles ahead of most people in our society. You don't have to be like many people who don't believe their lives or their work have meaning. You can have your highest need for meaning and purpose in life met because you belong to God and are made for His loving purpose.

I hope you'll choose what God wants for you, because it's the only path to reaching your true potential! The choices you make early in your life determine what you'll become in the future.

The View from Down Here

Thinking back over this chapter, review these ideas and fix them in your mind:

You were made in God's own image, so He could be reflected to all of creation through you. He made you to do kind, loving, helpful, and creative things for others, as He does.

Write down answers to these questions on a piece of paper you can tuck into this book:

1. Did you ever try to help someone become a Christian? Who? How?

2. Make a list of some good things you can do for someone to show him love. (Hints: Take your little brother out for ice cream. Wash the dishes so your mom can read a book. Mow the lawn before your dad asks. Invite someone lonely over to play games or listen to records.)

3. How do you spend your time? Are you "voting" for good?

4. If you have chosen a career, what kind of person might it cause you to become?

5

Sin—the Big Interruption

Humpty Dumpty wasn't the only one who had a great fall. We human types had a great fall too, because Adam and Eve chose to go Satan's way instead of God's. So sin entered the world and changed God's Creation. Man and the world were sabotaged. Because of sin, *nobody* can accurately know God or reflect His image until he's put back together again.

That's what God's man Paul told the Corinthians:

We can see and understand only a little about God now, as if we were peering at His reflection in a poor mirror; but someday we are going to see Him in His completeness, face to face. Now all that I know is hazy and blurred, but then I will see everything clearly, just as clearly as God sees into my heart right now (1 Corinthians 13:12, LB).

We have an antique mirror in our house. The frame is still golden and lovely, but the glass is splotchy and brown with age. My perception of myself is distorted when I look in that mirror. In the same way, our perception of God and our ability to reflect Him are distorted because sin puts blotches all over His reflection in us.

Just what is sin? Basically, sin is evil—it happens when a person chooses his own way instead of God's. Adam's disobedience made us all strangers to God. So we've inherited the *condition* of sin from him.

Sin is ugly. God hates it so much that He has to judge it and punish it. Sin interferes with His good plan for His creation, especially for people. Sin causes all the wretchedness and wickedness on earth. Even nature is waiting to be delivered from it (Romans 8:22).

Adam and the Sinful Core

Let's go back to the account of Adam's and Eve's first tussle with sin. God put them in a perfect environment with one no-no. Look what happened:

The serpent was the craftiest of all the creatures the Lord God had made. So the serpent came to the woman.

"Really?" he asked. "*None* of the fruit in the garden? God says you mustn't eat *any* of it?"

"Of course we may eat it," the woman told him. "It's only the fruit from the tree at the *center* of the garden that we are not to eat. God says we mustn't eat it or even touch it, or we will die."

"That's a lie!" the serpent hissed. "You'll not die! God knows very well that the instant you eat it you will become like Him, for your eyes will be opened—you will be able to distinguish good from evil!"

The woman was convinced. How lovely and fresh looking it was! And it would make her so wise! So she ate some of the fruit and gave some to her husband, and he ate it too. And as they ate it, suddenly they became aware of their nakedness, and were embarrassed. So they strung fig leaves together to cover themselves around the hips (Genesis 3:1-7, LB).

Are You Sure about That, God?

When the serpent Satan came to Eve, he immediately put doubt into her mind about God's good plan for her and Adam. He made her think God was keeping good things from them: knowledge and wisdom. (Satan still uses this trick, making people think God is keeping good things from them by asking them to be obedient.) Now there's nothing wrong with knowledge and wisdom, but Eve went about getting them in the wrong way. Instead of waiting to see what God would show her, she tried to get them her own way—by disobeying God's command. Sadly, Adam followed her lead. They got new knowledge all right—but look how immediately that knowledge worked against them:

That evening they heard the sound of the Lord God walking in the garden; and they hid themselves among the trees. The Lord God called to Adam, "Why are you hiding?"

And Adam replied, "I heard You coming and didn't want You to see me naked. So I hid."

"Who told you you were naked?" the Lord God asked. "Have you eaten fruit from the tree I warned you about?"

"Yes," Adam admitted, "but it was the woman You gave me who brought me some, and I ate it."

Then the Lord God asked the woman, "How could you do such a thing?"

"The serpent tricked me," she replied (Genesis 3:8-13, LB).

The Buck Didn't Stop There

Isn't it remarkable that their first act of disobedience made Adam and Eve feel guilty and caused them to hide from God? It took only one sin to make them feel uncomfortable with God! Immediately, they tried to wriggle out of the responsibility for their sin. Instead of repenting of their disobedience, Adam passed the buck and blamed it on Eve, and Eve blamed the serpent.

The Death Trap

This sin of disobedience had immediate results. God kept His word. Adam and Eve's sin led to spiritual death. They lost their sensitivity to God and their desire to follow Him completely. The most important and eternal part of God's likeness in them died. And that tragedy has affected everyone who has lived since then. You suffer because your spirit died through that sin too. That is why you are often "not OK" and you do your own will instead of God's.

When Adam sinned, sin entered the entire human

race. His sin spread death throughout all the world, so everything began to grow old and die, for all sinned. . . . For this one man, Adam, brought death to many through his *sin* (Romans 5:12, 15, LB).

Yes, Adam's sin caused death for everyone who has lived on earth, including you. But God made a way to overcome Adam's sin:

This one man, Jesus Christ, brought forgiveness to many through God's *mercy*. Adam's *one* sin brought the penalty of death to many, while Christ freely takes away *many* sins and gives glorious life instead. The sin of this one man, Adam, caused *death to be king over all*, but all who will take God's gift of forgiveness and acquittal are *kings of life* because of this one man, Jesus Christ. Yes, Adam's *sin* brought *punishment* to all, but Christ's *righteousness* makes men *right with God*, so that they can live. Adam caused many to be sinners because he *disobeyed* God, and Christ caused many to be made acceptable to God because He *obeyed*. The Ten Commandments were given so that all could see the extent of their failure to obey God's laws. But the more we see our sinfulness, the more we see God's abounding grace forgiving us (Romans 5:15-20, LB).

Kidnapped!

Scripture uses another comparison to illustrate what happened when sin entered the picture. Close your eyes and picture this. You are God's child, made by Him and for Him. You're having a fantastic time together. Then along comes some black-robed horseman, who snatches you up and takes you off to his own kingdom. Now instead of living in light and joy, you live in misery and darkness. A pretty grim picture, isn't it?

But that's not all! Picture the opposite happening. Your Father doesn't stand for your being kidnapped, so He sends your big Brother, Jesus, to get you back. He frees you, but while He is there, He gets killed in your place! (Would you refuse to leave because you've become used to the misery and darkness?)

> For [God] has rescued us out of the darkness and gloom of Satan's kingdom and brought us into the kingdom of His dear Son, who bought our freedom with His blood and forgave us all our sins (Colossians 1:13-14, LB).

We'll see in the next chapter exactly how God paid for sin through Jesus, so that we can be forgiven.

The View from Down Here

But before we talk more about God's plan to restore
and forgive you, think about these questions:

1. What things, attitudes, or habits do you see in
yourself which show that God's image in you is
messed up?

2. What things in your life show you have sin in
you?

3. Have you been restored to God's plan for you?

4. Do you want to have God forgive your sin and
restore you, so you can know Him and reflect Him as
He wants you to do?

6

God Came Through for You!

By deceiving Adam and Eve and causing them to disobey God, Satan made us all slaves of sin and death—both physical and spiritual death (Romans 6:23). We were captured by this enemy, even before we were born. But from the beginning, God promised to pay our ransom and bring us back to His own kingdom.

The Promise

Soon after Adam and Eve sinned, God promised them He'd send someone to crush Satan's power. Just before Jesus' birth Zacharias, the priest, prophesied, "Blessed be the Lord God of Israel, for He has visited us and accomplished redemption for His people" (Luke 1:68, NASB).

When Mary and Joseph took Jesus into the temple

to be circumcised on the eighth day as the Mosaic Law required, Simeon and Anna confirmed this prophecy. They recognized that Jesus was the promised Redeemer. (See Luke 2:29-32, 34-35, 38.)

Why Did God Wait?

Ever wonder why God waited so long to fulfill His promise? We can't know all the reasons, but one thing people learned by God's waiting was that mankind really needed a Rescuer. Old Testament writers tell of people's sins, failures, and ingratitude to their Creator. Even after God gave man His Law, nobody could keep it. So God made a temporary plan for forgiving sin—killing a lamb. (This sacrifice for sin was a preview of how Jesus would later die for us.)

But this temporary system didn't work too well. Old Testament sacrifices could make people outwardly clean, but they were not effective in cleansing people's inner consciences (Hebrews 9:13-14). So people lived with sin and fear. Nobody was exempt. But God had a plan. And when the time was right, He sent His Son into the world (Galatians 4:4). Jesus came to earth in a body like ours so He could communicate most clearly with people (Hebrews 2:14-17).

Since, then the children share in flesh and blood, He Himself likewise also partook of the same, that through death He might render powerless him who had the power of death, that is, the devil; and might deliver those who through fear of death were subject to slavery all their lives. For assuredly He does not give help to angels, but He gives help to the seed of Abraham. Therefore, He had to be made like His brethren in all things (Hebrews 2:14-17, NASB).

The Fear of Death

Jesus came to set us free from death and the *fear* of death. Consider some of the things people do because they fear death. In our culture, everyone wants to stay young, because becoming old means death is near. Even when someone dies, we try to deny death's effects by embalming the body and putting it in an elaborate box. People are afraid of death.

In other cultures too people are afraid of death. The Machiguengas of Peru are terrified when they hear wind whistling through jungle trees. They think it means evil spirits are coming to take them to death—and to an eternity of living with buzzards.

Dan Velie lived with the Orejones in Peru. One day while he and the chief were out fishing, the chief started to beat him. He apologized when he saw Dan's surprise.

"Oh, brother Dan, I have to beat you so the spirit of your wife's unborn baby won't cause bad luck or death on this trip," he explained.

Later, when another woman's baby died, Dan saw her kneel on the grave and receive a beating with nettles—again because of the fear of death.

"I have to beat her," the chief explained, "so the spirit of her baby doesn't return and cause more deaths." (Many years later this chief was delivered from his fear of death by believing in Jesus.)

God wants you to be delivered from sin, death, and fear. He ransomed you with His own Son, Jesus.

Though He was God, [He] did not demand and

cling to His rights as God, but laid aside His mighty power and glory, taking the disguise of a slave and becoming like men. And He humbled Himself even further, going so far as actually to die a criminal's death on a cross. Yet it was because of this that God raised Him up to the heights of heaven and gave Him a name which is above every other name (Philippians 2:6-9, LB).

God, the Creator of everything, took on human form and become subject to His own creation.

For God loved the world so much that He gave His only Son so that anyone who believes in Him shall not perish but have eternal life. God did not send His Son into the world to condemn it, but to save it (John 3:16-17, LB).

Worth More than $6 Million!

During the Crusades of the Middle Ages in the Holy Land, Moslems captured Richard the Lionhearted, king of England. They held him captive for many years while his country raised millions of dollars in gold and silver to get their king back. But their payment left the country bankrupt.

Today, world leaders and business executives are sometimes kidnapped and held for ransom. Sometimes their relatives pay millions of dollars to get them back. But God gave far more than $6 million to buy you back. He gave His own Son Jesus to pay the ransom for your sin.

God paid a ransom to save you from the impossible road to heaven which your fathers tried to take, and the ransom He paid was not mere gold or silver, as you very well know. But He paid for you with the precious lifeblood of Christ, the sinless, spotless Lamb of God. God chose Him for this purpose long before the world began, but only recently was He brought into public view, in these last days, as a blessing to you (1 Peter 1:18-20, LB).

Three Freedoms

When Jesus bought you back by dying for you, He won for you freedom from slavery to sin, from bondage to the Law, and from eternal death.

Freedom #1: Jesus conquered sin's power over you. You don't have to live under its power any longer.

You are still *tempted* by sin because of being in a sinful world. But if you're a Christian you don't have to give in to sin.

But remember this—the wrong desires that come into your life aren't anything new and different. Many others have faced exactly the same problems before you. And no temptation is irresistible. You can trust God to keep the temptation from becoming so strong that you can't stand up against it, for He has promised this and will do what He says. He will show you how to escape temptation's power so that you can bear up patiently against it (1 Corinthians 10:13, LB).

Your way of escape is the power of the Holy Spirit in you. Sometimes it is also wise to *run away* from temptation—to get out of its reach. (See 2 Timothy 2:22.) But if you do sin, God provides a way for you to be right with Him again:

> If we confess our sins to Him, He can be depended on to forgive us and to cleanse us from every wrong. (And it is perfectly proper for God to do this for us because Christ died to wash away our sins.) (1 John 1:9, LB)

Freedom #2: Jesus freed you from having to obey the rituals in the Law.

If you know Christ, God has freed you from the vicious circle of sin and death.

> We were slaves to Jewish laws and rituals for we thought they could save us. But when the right time came, the time God decided on, He sent his Son born of a woman, born as a Jew, to buy freedom for us who were slaves to the Law so that that He could adopt us as His very own sons (Galatians 4:3-5, LB).

Since it's impossible to fulfill the Law without God's Spirit, Jesus fulfilled it for you.

> We aren't saved from sin's grasp by knowing the commandments of God, because we can't and don't keep them, but God put into effect a different plan to save us. He sent His own Son in a human body like ours—except that ours are sinful—and destroyed sin's control over us by giving Himself as a sacrifice for our sins. So now we can obey God's laws if we follow after the Holy Spirit and no longer obey the old evil nature within us (Romans 8:3-4, LB).

Freedom #3: Since Jesus obeyed the Law perfectly for you, you don't have to die for your failure to obey it.

Yes, Jesus freed you from death! He broke "the power of death and showed us the way of everlasting life through trusting Him" (2 Timothy 1:10, LB). If you've received Christ as your Saviour, you will never have to experience separation from God.

What Does Freedom Mean?

Do you know how slaves lived in the early years of the United States? Perhaps you've seen the TV series "Roots" or read *Uncle Tom's Cabin*. Slavery was an ugly practice which many men died to change. But in the days of the Roman Empire, when the New Testament was written, slavery was even worse. A slave was totally at the mercy of his owner.

Without the freedom Jesus gives us, we're like slaves, totally at the mercy of sin and death.

In New Testament days, a good master could choose to give freedom to his slaves. Or someone else could buy a slave and set him free. Then the slave would have a totally new life.

But sometimes a slave loved his master or the one who freed him so much that even after he was set free, he remained a slave. He *voluntarily* stayed with the one he loved.

This is the picture Scripture gives about your relationship either to sin or to God. Even though Jesus has paid for your freedom, you may choose to keep sin as your master, because you like sin. But if you accept the freedom Jesus gives you from sin, you can voluntarily give yourself to Him, to serve Him rather than sin.

New Humanity

To be a new person means to have God's Spirit in you. Paul says, "If any man is in Christ, he is a new creature; the old things passed away; behold, new things have come" (2 Corinthians 5:17, NASB). You become newly sensitive to God, to people, to nature. In his book *They Dared to Be Different*, Hugh Steven gives a beautiful example of someone becoming a new person. Mariano, a Chamula Indian of Mexico, grew up in bitter circumstances and suffered from harsh treatment. He had little hope of breaking out of the prison which his restrictive culture and his drunken father had made for him. But then he heard of Christ and the new life He offered. Mariano accepted Christ's love. He was changed! He became a new man, restored to the beauty and sensitivity for which God had made him.

What about You?

Maybe you're wondering how you can become a new creature. It's really simple. God offers to make *anyone* new who comes to Him, since Jesus has already paid the price. "For by grace you have been saved through faith; and that not of yourselves, it is the gift of God; not as a result of works, that no one should boast" (Ephesians 2:8-9, NASB).

After you receive God's freely offered salvation, nothing can separate you from His love. Satan can't separate you from God either. When Jesus died, He took away your sin—and Satan's power over you.

So if you admit that you're sinful and accept what Jesus did for you, you become a new person in Christ. And when you give your life to Him, a whole new world opens up before you. God has a lot planned for you!

If you've never asked Christ to come into your life before, maybe you'd like to stop right now and ask Him. Pray a simple prayer. Tell Him you're sinful and you accept His death for you. Tell Him you want to have your sins forgiven and become His child.

Accept Jesus—Accept Yourself

God's forgiveness is the basis for forgiving yourself. You're forgiven and free. In Christ you have new power to be and do what pleases God. (This includes forgiving people who have hurt you. Since God has forgiven you, you can afford to forgive them.)

Because sin still pulls on you, you will sometimes fall. *But—you don't have to stay down.* Because you can confess your sins and be forgiven, you can get up and get going again.

Suppose you have a rotten temper. After you accept Jesus, you really blow it and argue with your best friend. Do you have to avoid him because you feel ashamed? No way. You can admit you were wrong and ask your friend and God to forgive you. Because you know God forgives you, you can forgive yourself and keep growing in your Christian life. For you died to sin with Jesus on the cross, and He raised you up with Him to live His new life.

What's This Got to Do with Self-Esteem?

Understanding all this about sin-death-power-freedom is crucial to *how* you see yourself. Many psychologists and psychiatrists say people want to believe they're good, but they feel an evil pull that makes them do bad things. This dual nature makes them feel depressed because they don't know if they are good or bad.

This is where you have a great advantage. As a Christian, you can make an honest self-appraisal. Because you understand sin, you can feel its pull in your life. And because you understand what God has done to free you, you can ignore that pull. And rising above that tendency to sin helps your self-image.

A Christian can admit the extent of his sin, because he has a way to handle it. If a nonbeliever admits how bad he really is, he is more apt to be crushed by that shocking knowledge. His self-esteem may fall apart because he can't get rid of his guilt. He has no remedy for his sin.

When you understand sin, you can understand your failures. But you aren't stuck with them. Because God forgives you, you can forgive yourself—and keep going in *God's power*.

The View from Down Here

Answer these questions to review this chapter:

1. How much am I worth to God? How much did He pay to win me back?

2. Why don't I have to be afraid of eternal death?

3. If I'm a new person in Christ, how does God see me?

4. How can accepting God's forgiveness improve my self-esteem?

If you're a new person in Christ, all the rest of this book is about you. It gives more reasons why you're special!

7

You're Not Just a Face in the Crowd

The dean of girls at my high school called me in to tell me I'd been chosen to go to Girls' State, a program sponsored by the American Legion Auxiliary for training high school girls in democractic leadership. I was excited and exhilarated! *I* had been chosen for a special privilege and honor. I didn't waste any time telling my mom and my friends.

Later, I was chosen to receive a college scholarship. That was exciting too. But the most exciting time of my life was when Larry asked me to be his wife. That was awesome, thrilling.

We all want to be chosen—as a friend, as a team member, as a lover. Perhaps you've dreamed of being chosen homecoming queen, or captain of the football team. But do you know that *God* wants you? He wants you to become His son or daughter.

You're a Child of God

As 1 child in a family of 12 children, I used to dream about being adopted. I thought it would be special to be chosen by someone, instead of just happening to be born into a big family. I used to dream about belonging to a doctor's family, living in a two-story house, and having a ruffled bedspread. I didn't know then that I'd been chosen by God.

Our friend Hobart has an adopted son who got quite upset one day when he was about eight years old.

"What's the matter, Son?" Hobart asked him.

"I don't want to be adopted! I want to be your real son!" he said.

"Oh," his dad said. "So that's the problem. Well let me see. . . ." Hobart thought fast and prayed for wisdom.

"Listen, Son, it's OK to be adopted. Did you know I'm adopted too?"

"Really? I didn't know that!"

"Yep," Hobart said. "I'm adopted by God. He wanted another son and He chose me, as I chose you to be my son."

"OK, Dad. That's OK!"

From the beginning God wanted to make you holy, to be clean and pure and not to let sin mess up your life. Paul says, "[God] chose us in Him before the foundation of the world, that we should be holy and blameless before Him. In love He predestined us to adoption as sons" (Ephesians 1:4-5, NASB).

You—God's Friend

Did you ever wish you could be really "in" with a certain group of people? I have. You feel a strange kind of loneliness when you don't belong, when you're not part of the popular group.

But here's good news for you! If you're a Christian, you're part of God's "in-group." When Jesus made His farewell speech and prayed for His disciples, He told them:

> You are My friends, if you do what I command you. No longer do I call you slaves; for the slave does not know what his master is doing; but I have called you friends, for all things that I have heard from My Father I have made known to you. You did not choose Me, but I chose you, and appointed you, that you should go and bear fruit, and that your fruit should remain; that whatever you ask of the Father in My name, He may give to you (John 15:14-16, NASB).

Jesus made this promise to you and me as well as to the 12 disciples. (See John 17:20.) So you can read this sentence to yourself:

"I, _____ , if I belong to Jesus, am a friend of God the Father. Jesus is my Friend and Brother." (See Hebrews 2:11.)

God Himself chose you to be His companion and friend. You have the privilege of talking, walking, and living with Him. The more time you spend with Him, the more you will become like Him.

You—God's Inheritance

Larry and I recently inherited a lovely quilt made by Larry's great grandmother about 125 years ago.

Usually the things we inherit have special meaning for us. Is there something you look forward to inheriting someday? If so, it means you will have some special tie with that object because of its age or the person who passed it on.

God always makes it clear that His most special treasures are people. Through the psalmist, God speaks of you as His inheritance: "Blessed is the nation whose God is the Lord, the people whom He has chosen for His own inheritance" (Psalm 33:12, NASB).

This was first written to Israel, but it also applies to us. We were made an inheritance for Jesus. One translation says "We too were made His heritage" (Ephesians 1:11, BERK).

You're not an antique yet—but you're already a priceless part of God's inheritance!

Chosen—for Angel Protection

God sends His angels to protect us, and sometimes to lead us to Him. God says the angels are "spiritual messengers sent out to help and care for those who are to receive His salvation" (Hebrews 1:14, LB).

Some people have had dramatic experiences of God's protection. Take Wilf, for instance. One day he was walking in the woods of British Columbia, tripped out on drugs, when the railroad tracks started moving wildly and a wind swirled around him, beating the trees furiously.

"Lie down on the tracks and die!" he heard voices say to him. "Commit suicide! Die!" He felt evil spirits surrounding him.

Wilf was scared. He remembered having heard as a boy that it was wrong to commit suicide.

"God, if there is a God, help me!" he called out. "Bring me back to my right mind!"

Immediately, he regained his senses. He felt the presence of good spirits.

"Read the Bible," they seemed to say to him. "It will help you."

So Wilf did, and he came to know Jesus. (You can read Wilf's story in *The Sower*, April 1979, published by the World Home Bible League.)

After we become Christians, God's angels continue to take care of us. They surround us to protect us. (See Psalms 34:7 and 91:11.) We're not always aware of God's protection, but it's still real.

Once our Grandfather Dodds was driving along the Pacific Coast near Malibu. The fog was thick. As he inched along in his old Franklin, the wheel suddenly spun in his hands and turned the car sharply to the right. Shaken, he stopped the car and got out to look. He'd just been saved from driving over a 50-foot cliff into the ocean!

Besides protecting you, the angels minister to you at times of crisis in your life. God sent an angel to guide Israel through the desert (Exodus 23:20-23). When Daniel was in the lions' den, angels shut the lions' mouths so they couldn't attack him (Daniel 6:22).

When the Prophet Elijah was so discouraged that he ran away to the wilderness, God sent an angel to give him hot bread and water (1 Kings 19:5-7).

While Jesus was being tempted for 40 days and nights, Satan tried to get Him to throw Himself off the top of the temple.

Satan taunted, "[God] will give His angels charge concerning You; and on their hands they will bear You up, lest You strike Your foot against a stone" (Matthew 4:6, NASB).

Jesus, of course, knew the angels would protect Him. But He also knew the promise hadn't been made so He could show off His power. Later, God sent His angels to minister to Jesus in other ways (Mark 1:13).

Jesus prayed that the Father would keep us safe from Satan's power too (John 17:15). His own experience with Satan made Him even more aware that we need to be protected from Satan.

Maybe you're faced with a big temptation, or some tough situation. You can *know* that God will protect you and help you, if you're one of His children.

The View from Down Here

Answer these questions to help you focus on how these ideas apply to you:

1. Do your attitudes and conduct show that God has chosen you? How?

2. What are you doing to cultivate your friendship with God? Is it a mutual friendship or all one-sided?

3. How can you make your friendship with God deeper? (Think about some things He has done for you. Can you do any of them for Him?)

4. Can you think of any times when God protected you or comforted you in some special way? Have you ever told Him "Thank You"?

8

You Are God's Home

While living in Peru, we've had visitors in our home from every social class and from many countries. It's been exciting to have ambassadors from various countries come for dinner or spend the weekend. Before someone visits, I shine and polish everything. I cut fresh flowers and make the house as beautiful as I can.

But all this is trivial, compared with who lives inside of me—and you—every day. If you're a Christian, God, the Creator of everything, has chosen to make you His home. Jesus told His disciples, "I will ask the Father, and He will give you another Counselor to be with you forever—the Spirit of Truth. The world cannot accept Him, because it neither sees Him nor knows Him. But you know Him, for He lives with you and will be in you" (John 14:16-17, NIV).

A Trinity Mystery House

As Christians, most of us know that the Holy Spirit lives in us. But do you know that the Father and the Son Jesus also live in you? Because the Trinity—the Father, the Son, and the Holy Spirit—is One, all three members live in you.

Jesus spoke often of how the Father and He are One (John 10:30; 14:10, 20). Paul reminds us of this too. "God was reconciling the world to Himself in Christ" (2 Corinthians 5:19, NIV). "For in Christ all the fullness of the Deity lives in bodily form" (Colossians 2:9, NIV).

Jesus promised that when someone believes in Him, He and the Father will come to live with that person (John 14:23).

John summarizes this complex relationship well.

> No one has beheld God at any time; if we love one another, God abides in us, and His love is perfected in us. By this we know that we abide in Him and He in us, because He has given us of His Spirit. And we have beheld and bear witness that the Father has sent the Son to be the Saviour of the world. Whoever confesses that Jesus is the Son of God, God abides in him, and he in God. And we have come to know and have believed the love which God has for us. God is love, and the one who abides in love abides in God, and God abides in him (1 John 4:12-16, NASB).

I wish I'd understood how Jesus lives in me when I was a teenager. I would have spent more time praying "Lord, You do this (or that) *through* me," rather than praying, "Lord, make me better" or "Lord, help me do this." I would have been able to relax more if I had known He wants to live through me, instead of my having to try so hard to live His life.

What about Your Body?

Jesus sent the Holy Spirit to live in believers on the Day of Pentecost. He's lived in believers ever since.

> Don't you realize that you yourselves are the temple of God, and that God's Spirit lives in you? God will destroy anyone who defiles His temple, for His temple is holy—*and that is exactly what you are!* (1 Corinthians 3:16-17, PH)

> Avoid sexual looseness like the plague! . . . Have you forgotten that . . . you are not the owner of your own body? You have been bought, and at what a price! Therefore, bring glory to God both in your body and in your spirit, for they both belong to Him (1 Corinthians 6:18-20, PH).

That's pretty straight talk! Because God has bought you and given you His Spirit, He cares about what you do with your body, as well as with your spirit. He becomes jealous when sin separates you from Him (James 4:5).

God has given life to you through His Spirit living in you (Romans 8:10). He wants you to take good care of your life—and your body—because they are His gifts to you. Because He lives in you, He wants you to be pure.

Respecting your body as God's temple means keeping it healthy and attractive. Anything that doesn't contribute to your health violates God's temple. Overeating, or eating the wrong kinds of foods, for instance, ruins both your health and your appearance. Staying up late and sleeping too little hurt your body too.

What we see, what we take into the body through our eyes, affects the health of our whole being. In the Sermon on the Mount, Jesus said, "The lamp of the body is the eye; if therefore your eye is clear, your whole body will be full of light. But if your eye is bad, your whole body will be full of darkness" (Matthew 6:22-23, NASB).

Your eye is like a camera for your mind. It records what it sees and stores it for future replay. The books you read, the TV and movies you watch, and the other things your eyes dwell on affect your spiritual and physical health. It's a mistake to think you can be so sophisticated that what you see has no effect on you. You can't expose yourself to bad scenes without losing some of your purity.

Because you're God's temple, you can't afford to take alcohol and other drugs or harmful substances into your body. These things not only harm your body, but they also distort your mind and spirit. If you keep in mind that you're special because God Himself lives in you, you'll think too much of yourself to take foolish risks.

Many studies have shown that it's people with low self-esteem who indulge in dangerous and harmful practices. Since they think they're not worth much, they figure they've little to lose by gambling with their lives. People with good self-images and high self-esteem, however, believe they're too valuable to risk damaging themselves.

Your body is a beautiful and intricate gift of God. If you're a Christian it houses the most incredible treasure: God's own Spirit in your personality. Care for your body as a gift you give back to God daily. Make the most of the good gifts He has given you.

What the Holy Spirit Does for You

With the Holy Spirit living in you, you have the most fantastic resource in the world. He's one resource you'll still have long after the world runs out of oil, gas, and even solar power.

Look what the Holy Spirit is for you:

1. *Your Comforter.* Jesus said, "He [God] will give you another Comforter" (John 14:16, LB).

2. *Your Truth and Guide.* The Spirit of Truth will guide you (John 16:13).

3. *Your Teacher.* "The Helper, the Holy Spirit, whom the Father will send in My name, He will teach you all things, and bring to your remembrance all that I said to you" (John 14:26, NASB).

4. *Your Intercessor.* The Holy Spirit *prays* for you: "The Spirit also helps our weakness; for we do not know how to pray as we should, but the Spirit Himself intercedes for us with groanings too deep for words; and He who searches the hearts knows what the mind of the Spirit is, because He intercedes for the saints according to the will of God" (Romans 8:26-27, NASB).

5. *Your Strength.* "He would grant you, according to the riches of His glory, to be strengthened with power through His Spirit in the inner man" (Ephesians 3:16, NASB).

6. *Your Purifier.* "But you were washed, but you were sanctified, but you were justified in the name of the Lord Jesus Christ, and in the Spirit of our God" (1 Corinthians 6:11, NASB).

7. *Your Seal of Salvation.* The Holy Spirit is the

guarantee, or down payment, of your salvation, to prove that God will complete it when Jesus returns and takes you to heaven with Him. Since you still live in your body in a sinful world, your salvation hasn't been completed yet. "Having also believed, you were sealed in Him with the Holy Spirit of promise" (Ephesians 1:13, NASB).

Life in the Vine

Jesus uses a beautiful analogy to describe your life in Him and His life in you. He says that He is the Vine, and believers are the branches (John 15). Picture a vine in your mind—maybe a grapevine. See the soil line? Above that is a low, twisted vine with branches, leaves, and fruit. Below the soil are the roots, which you can't see. Yet the vine couldn't live without them. It would dry up and topple over.

Your roots—and mine—are supposed to grow in God's love. We are to sink our roots deep into the soil of His love (Ephesians 3:17). If your roots are secure, your vine will be healthy.

You can tell a grapevine from a watermelon vine because of the fruit it produces. When you are in the Christ-vine, you bear a certain kind of fruit. And, as with the grapevine, your fruit grows from the life of the vine flowing through you, not from your trying to grow fruit.

Here is the cluster of fruit God says will grow in your life when you are in Him: love, joy, peace, patience, kindness, goodness, faithfulness, gentleness, self-control (Galatians 5:22-23).

In contrast, look at the fruit of the "self-sin vine": sexual immorality, impurity and debauchery, sensuality, idolatry, witchcraft, hatred, discord, jealousy, fits of rage, selfish ambition, dissensions, factions, envy, drunkenness, orgies (Galatians 5:19-21). Not the kind of fruit you need!

The fruit of the Spirit reflects God's characteristics. So you reflect God by growing His fruit in your life. You grow His fruit by letting Jesus live through you. You don't have to worry about developing God's fruit by yourself! The Holy Spirit does it for you if you let Him control you.

Let's think more about this fruit. What does God say here about intelligence, status, and education? Nothing! Why not? God puts the emphasis on what you *are*, rather than on what you *do*. So it's possible to have spiritual fruit in your life even if you're not highly intelligent, beautiful, well-educated, or "successful." The only requirement is to let Jesus' Spirit live in and through you. That's good news!

I've seen this work in the lives of some simple people. One Easter, we went to the home of Doña Sarah, a Quechua woman who lives in the foothills of the Andes Mountains. She's probably never been to school and she's very poor. But as we sat in her dirt-floored house, eating from metal bowls, we saw Jesus living through her. She had all that lovely spiritual fruit growing in her life, because she had learned how to live in Jesus.

In the same way, you can bear God's fruit in your life. Even if you live a simple life and don't achieve much by the world's standards, you can reflect God to the people in your school, your home, and your city if you bear His fruit.

Of Pinecones and Cherries

My family and I are in the Sierra Nevada Mountains as I write this chapter. We passed miles of grapevines as we drove through the central valley of California. But now we are surrounded by pine, cedar, sequoia, and other trees. The ground is covered with their cones in some places.

I've been thinking about pinecones, grapes, and the fruit of the Spirit. Each has two functions: to reproduce and to give food. When you show love, joy, and peace other people want to know God because of you. As a Christian, you reproduce by planting seeds in their lives so that they come to know Christ. And when you love people, are patient with them, and use your fruit in other ways in their lives, you feed their emotions and their spirits. They taste God through *your* fruit and get an idea of what He is like because of you.

A funny experience helped me understand this concept. Some friends gave us a tiny cherry tree. For weeks it sat in a gallon can on the porch because I couldn't get around to planting it. One day Michael came in, smelling like cherries.

"Ummm," I said. "Where did you get the cherries?"

"Off our tree," he told me.

"Really? Off our little tree?" I asked.

"Yep," he said, so I had to go look for myself.

Sure enough, our little tree had two bright red cherries on it. Even though it was only two feet tall, the cherries it produced were red and fragrant. No one could ever mistake it for an apple tree. In the same way, you can bear God's fruit before you are fully mature.

Yes, you live in God, and He lives in you. You can feel excited about yourself and take care of yourself, because you are more important than the most elegant cathedral in the world! You are God's home!

The View from Down Here

Find a juicy apple or some other fruit and eat it while you answer these questions:

1. Do you believe that God lives in you?

2. If so, how do you take care of your body, His home?

3. Do you ever grieve the Holy Spirit by not respecting yourself, His temple?

4. Write down some of the nice qualities of the fruit you're eating. What do you notice about it? How does it compare with *you?*

5. Which of the cluster of spiritual fruit are most obvious in your life? Which spiritual fruit are least obvious?

6. What can you do to share God's fruit with more people?

I, GOD, do
to my
love, patience, hope,
eternal life...
bequeath
children

9

You'll Never Believe What You're Going to Inherit!

Howard Hughes was said to be one of the wealthiest men in the world. People wondered who would inherit his riches and how much there was to inherit. Sadly, he had no loving friend or relative to leave his fortune to.

Someday you'll inherit the wealth of Someone far richer than Mr. Hughes. Because God made you His child, you're an heir of many things. Your inheritance is based on your place in the family of God.

If we are His children we share His treasures, and all that Christ claims as His will belong to all of us as well! Yes, if we share in His sufferings we shall certainly share in His glory. In my opinion whatever we may have to go through now is less than nothing compared with the magnificent future God has planned for us. The whole creation is on tiptoe to see the wonderful sight of the sons of God coming into their own (Romans 8:17-20, PH).

Through the Son God made the whole universe, and to the Son He has ordained that all creation shall ultimately belong (Hebrews 1:2, PH).

Since everything belongs to Jesus, you (if you're a Christian) are His co-heir, and will someday share in a huge inheritance. This includes things in the physical world, and all aspects of the spiritual realm. Can you feel poor when you think about being a joint-heir with God's Son?

What Do You Inherit?

Let's look at our inheritance:

● **God's promises.** In the Old Testament, God made an agreement with His friend Abraham. God said He'd send a Saviour to redeem His people. This promise is for us too (Galatians 3:29).

This promise of salvation is only one of hundreds

that God has made to you. If you want to know more than 800 other promises, read David Wilkerson's *Promises to Live By*, published by Regal Books.

● **Eternal life.** Instead of eternal death as punishment for your sins, God gives you an eternal life that begins the minute you trust in Christ. Just think: Your life on earth is just a fraction of your *total life!*

Because of His great kindness . . . we can share in the wealth of the eternal life He gives us, and we are eagerly looking forward to receiving it (Titus 3:7, LB).

● **Righteousness.** Paul became an heir of righteousness because of his faith in God's Word. That means he inherited God's right-ness (Philippians 3:9).

If you're a genuine Christian, God sees you through the goodness and perfection of Jesus. And, depending on how faithful to Him you are, God will reward you with gifts, which the Bible calls "crowns." These gifts will be precious to you, yet you'll want to give them back to Jesus as an expression of how much you love Him (Revelation 4:10-11).

● **God's kingdom.** Close your eyes and imagine what it would be like to be a member of a royal family in a peaceful kingdom. Your father, the king, will someday pass his kingdom on to you. You have the best of everything. People bow to you and come to you for important decisions. It's a pretty neat picture, isn't it?

God says Christians will inherit a kingdom someday (Matthew 25:34). Your Father, God, is Ruler over all, and He has a kingdom which Jesus often spoke of. (For example, see Matthew 25:31-36.)

Someday you'll reign with Christ. John, whom Jesus loved so much, writes about this new kingdom in the Book of Revelation:

> There shall be nothing in the city which is evil; for the throne of God and of the Lamb will be there, and His servants will worship Him. And they shall see His face; and His name shall be written on their foreheads. And there will be no night there—no need for lamps or sun—for the Lord God will be their light; and they shall reign forever and ever (Revelation 22:3-5, LB).

God will reward you according to what you've done with the gifts, abilities, and opportunities He gave you. He will evaluate your life from a spiritual, eternal point of view. Your material or worldly success won't matter to Him. How much you've done to build His kindgom will. (If you want to know more about God's rewards for you, study the following passages: 1 Corinthians 9:25; Ephesians 6:8; Colossians 3:23-25; Revelation 22:12.)

A Self-Fulfilling Prophecy?

Psychologists and teachers often talk about "self-fulfilling prophecies." They mean that when we *believe* something will happen, it affects the way we act and think, which usually causes it to happen.

For instance, if your dad thinks you're dumb and tells you so every day, chances are you'll believe it and not use your intelligence. You'll probably end up making his "prophecy" come true.

Do you remember that I said I wanted to belong to

a doctor's family, live in a two-story house, and have a ruffled bedspread? This was a "self-fulfilling prophecy" for me. I married a doctor and got a ruffled bedspread. When we designed our own house in the jungle, we made it with an upstairs!

Related to this idea of a self-fulfilling prophecy is what some psychologists call a "life script." We tend to live out the kind of life we think we will live out. This concept applies to your life with God too. When you know what God says about you and that you can follow His plan for you, you are able to live out His "script" for you. When you remind yourself that you are His son and heir, it affects what you think and do. The more you obey God, the more He honors you, and the better you feel about yourself.

I like to think about this as a "God-fulfilling prophecy" because He makes it come true. The more you cooperate with Him and act out what He says you are, the sooner you'll see that it's true. The more you let His Spirit control you, the more you'll become like Him, and the greater your reward will be.

I practice this principle as a missionary. God has promised to take care of all my needs—for time, for energy, for patience, for love, and for material things. He even promises to give me enough so I can be generous with other people! So I visualize what I need, and trust God to give it to me. And do you know what? I always have everything I really need! Because God is my Father and He's rich in all things, I trust Him and He takes care of me.

When you know what you'll inherit with Christ, you'll feel rich too. You won't have to be afraid of people, or feel bad if they put you down. You won't have to worry about today or tomorrow or the future. You can seek God's kingdom first and know that He'll give you everything else that you'll need. (Read Matthew 6:24-34 to see how He'll take care of you.)

The View from Down Here

1. Make a list of the benefits, other than material possessions, God has given to you.

2. Write down some of the things you believe about yourself. How are you making these things come true?

3. Do you want to *change* some of the things you are making come true, so that they will be closer to God's view of you? Which ones? Share these with a friend and pray together about them.

10

Believe It or Not, You're a Priest

People in almost every culture have a priest or "shaman" to stand between them and their god. They believe this special person has some spiritual power or special access to at least one god. This special priest represents the people to a god by offering sacrifices, saying prayers, and performing rituals. He speaks for the god to the people as he gets messages through visions, dreams, or oracles.

The priest is respected, even held in awe. He doesn't live just for himself; he has a duty to fulfill.

In the Old Testament, God set up a special order of priests for the Israelites, His chosen people. The priests were men from the Levite tribe. They performed special duties in order to help the people in their relationships with God.

The most important priest of all was the high priest. It was his privilege—and only his—to go into the most sacred part of the temple, the Holy of Holies, once a year to sprinkle blood on the altar so God would forgive the people's sins. In order to be completely pure, the priest had to make special preparations for cleansing his mind, his body, and even his clothes. His priestly robe had bells sewed to the bottom of it, so other priests could hear him moving about inside the Holy of Holies. If a high priest didn't live a holy life, it meant death for him. Some historical sources say he also had a rope tied to his ankle. If he was unworthy and God struck him dead, his body could be pulled out.

Jesus Is Our High Priest

"Christ redeemed us from the curse of the [Old Testament] Law by becoming a curse for us" (Galatians 3:13, NIV). He made it possible for us to be saved by trusting in His death and resurrection. Jesus became our High Priest.

> But Jesus the Son of God is our great High Priest who has gone to heaven itself to help us; therefore let us never stop trusting Him. This High Priest of ours understands our weaknesses, since He had the same temptations we do, though He never once gave way to them and sinned. So let us come boldly to the very throne of God and stay there to receive His mercy and to find grace to help us in our times of need (Hebrews 4:14-16, LB).

At the time of Jesus' death, the huge cloth veil in the temple which separated the Holy of Holies from the rest of the temple tore from top to bottom. In this way, God symbolized that He was accessible to everyone. Now, instead of being available only to the high priest, God was inviting all His people to come directly to Him.

You Are God's Priest

Because Jesus prepared the way for you, you can go directly to God on behalf of yourself and other people. You have become God's priest (1 Peter 2:5). You don't have to have someone else stand between you and God. You can even pray for people and plead their causes before God.

When you pray for someone, you help to bring about God's will for him. I hope you like this role God has given you. Through it you can accomplish great things for His kingdom! Has God ever helped any of your friends because you asked Him to? I hope so!

I've always marveled at how God protected me during my childhood. I am one of 12 children; we had tremendous problems in our home. As a result, my brothers and sisters have experienced tragedies in their lives. From an early age, I knew God and had a strong desire to please Him. So many of the things that should've made me abnormal didn't.

Once when I was sharing this with a pastor friend and my husband Larry, Larry told about his parents' teaching when he was a boy. From the time he was four years old, they taught him to pray for the girl who would someday be his wife.

Our pastor friend became excited.

"That's it, Lois! Don't you see that it's because Larry was praying for you all during your childhood that God protected you from all those dangers? God honored Larry's prayers for you, even though Larry was just a little child. He prayed in faith, and God answered his prayers!"

We looked at each other, amazed. We knew it must be true. Larry is four years older than I, so from the time of my birth he was praying for me, and God took care of me in special ways.

You have the same kind of potential as God's priest. Have you ever considered praying for your future mate? I believe God will answer your prayers, and lead you to the person He knows will be best for you.

I've acted as a priest for many people too. I think especially of my friend Chris. We met in a night class at the local college, while studying existentialism. Chris is a dynamic person, with strong beliefs and a strong personality. Immediately, I loved her and wanted her to know God. At the time, she was far from Him. But because she had a high regard for truth, she was willing to talk with me.

During the next year we became close friends as we discussed God's viewpoint of life and truth. I prayed for her constantly because I wanted her to know God, and I believed that when she was convinced about Him and His love for her, all her energy and drive would be redirected toward loving and serving Him. I knew she would find an exciting purpose for her life. And that's just what happened. A year later, Chris accepted Christ. She became a new person and changed in beautiful ways. God has given her a tremendous ministry teaching hundreds of women in a large Bible class each week. Because I've prayed for her over the last 12 years, I share in that ministry. God honored my prayers—and her desire to follow Him.

Chris has also become an important priest of God for me. Because of her daily prayers for me, God has given me strength and courage to serve Him in the jungle. He's rescued me from many difficulties because of Chris' faithful prayers and her sound advice. Thus, she shares in all my ministry, as I share in hers.

I know I'm a priest, so I feel responsible for keeping my life pure. I wouldn't want to mess up or forfeit my priest-role because of sin. It would be awful if my sin kept me from speaking God's Word to someone, or praying for him. I hope you take this seriously too. Wouldn't it be tragic if someone you loved didn't find salvation because of sin in your life? God wants you to live a pure life because you're His priest and He trusts you with His message.

Worship — Your Priestly Privilege

One of your special privileges as a priest is to worship God, to offer Him praise and adoration. Have you ever noticed how you glow inside when someone you love tells you that you're wonderful? You love to hear praise and appreciation, especially from someone close to you.

You probably appreciate it most when someone praises you for your qualities, rather than just for what you do for him. When someone praises you, it builds you up. When you praise and worship God, you magnify Him. You bring Him glory.

Praising someone always renews your own appreciation of that person. So it is with God. Praising Him reminds you how great He is!

God deserves all the praise and adoration you can give Him—and more! Here is how Jesus will be worshiped some day, as the Apostle John tells us in the Book of Revelation:

> The 24 elders fell down before the Lamb, each with a harp and golden vials filled with incense— the prayers of God's people! They were singing Him a new song with these words: "You are worthy to take the scroll and break its seals and open it; for You were slain, and Your blood has bought people from every nation as gifts for God. And You have gathered them into a kingdom and made them priests of our God; they shall reign upon the earth." Then in my vision I heard the singing of millions of angels surrounding the throne and the living beings and the elders: "The Lamb is worthy" (loudly they sang it!) "—the Lamb who was slain. He is worthy to receive the power, and the riches, and the wisdom, and the strength, and the honor, and the glory, and the blessing."
>
> And then I heard everyone in heaven and earth, and from the dead beneath the earth and in the sea, exclaiming, "The blessing and the honor and the glory and the power belong to the One sitting on the throne, and to the Lamb forever and ever" (Revelation 5:8-13, LB).

You'll worship God for eternity. You'll reign as His priest forever. How can you prepare yourself for that role now?

The View from Down Here

1. Is there someone in your life—at school or at home—for whom you can act as a priest?

2. What can you ask God for this person?

3. What message of God's can you give that person?

4. In what ways do you worship God, and let Him know how great He is? What more can you do to let Him know you love Him?

11

Jesus Gives You Share-Power

Can you imagine hiking up in the mountains with your best friend? You climb over rocks and crunch pine needles beneath your boots. You jump little gullies and drink from a gurgling creek. At last you reach the top of a mountain and drop down onto a sunny spot to look out over the valley below. The sun is warm on your back, and the breeze is cool on your face. You reach into your backpack and pull out a Hershey bar. Do you eat it alone? Chances are you share it with your friend. You're glad to be there together, sharing the climb and view. Something's really strange if you don't share your chocolate too.

What You Share with Jesus

When Jesus came to earth to live with us and die for us, He was one of us. He showed us how to have a warm, living relationship with the Father. And He also shared many of our characteristics.

● **Flesh and blood.** Jesus, as God in heaven, had never before experienced life as a flesh and blood person. He became human for us.

Since we, God's children, are human beings— made of flesh and blood—He became flesh and blood too by being born in human form; for only as a human being could He die and in dying break the power of the devil who had the power of death (Hebrews 2:14, LB).

● **Suffering.** Before Jesus came to earth, He didn't experience physical suffering or affliction. But He shared in this part of our humanity too. So we aren't alone in pain and sorrow.

Dear friends, don't be bewildered or surprised when you go through the fiery trials ahead, for this is no strange, unusual thing that is going to happen to you. Instead, be really glad—because these trials will make you partners with Christ in His suffering, and afterwards you will have the wonderful joy of sharing His glory in that coming day when it will be displayed (1 Peter 4:12-13, LB).

Even when Paul was in jail, he could tell Timothy not to be afraid of suffering: "You will be ready to suffer with me for the Lord, for He will give you strength in suffering," Paul said. "Take your share of suffering as a good soldier of Christ, just as I do. I am comforted . . . that when we suffer and die for Christ it only means that we will begin living with Him in heaven" (2 Timothy 1:8; 2:3, 11, LB).

Paul said that we are allowed to suffer so we can learn about God's comfort and encouragement. Then we can share it with others. (See 1 Peter 5:10-11.)

In Paul's day and in many countries today, suffering *for* Christ was and is real. In some places being a Christian means being ridiculed, imprisoned, or even put to death. But there is another sense in which we suffer *with* Christ. Because Jesus is love, He cares about people. He gave up His own life to save mankind. So if you have the mind of Christ, you'll suffer when people reject Him. You'll hate sin and the ruin it brings into people's lives. If you suffer with Christ in these areas, you'll want to change your world. You'll want to take away Jesus' suffering—and people's—by sharing His love with them.

When you know you belong to God, you can cope with the suffering of disease and death too. Scott, a close friend of my son David, became ill with Hodgkin's disease when he was just 10. He lived for four years, though doctors predicted he would live only two. He courageously endured all the suffering his illness and his treatments caused. He had incredible patience. He never gave up hope or his zest for life. He loved life and enthusiastically pursued many interests in spite of his illness. Because of his faith in God, he never gave in to despair. Scott knew who he was, and though he wanted to go on living, he died with a courage and dignity that many adults never know. He enriched the lives of many people in his few short years of life.

(You can read Scott's story in *Scott Was Here*, by Elaine Ipswitch, Delacorte Press, New York, 1979.)

● **Temptation.** Jesus also experienced temptation, probably the most painful aspect of our humanity.

Before He took on a human body and became subject to physical death by living in a sinful world, Jesus didn't have to struggle with the pull of sin. But on earth, He suffered every temptation that you and I do. When you tell Jesus of your temptation, you know He'll understand because He faced a similar temptation. And because He didn't sin when He was tempted, He can give you power to resist it (Hebrews 4:15-16).

What Jesus Shares with You

When you understand that you share in Jesus' godliness as He shared in your humanness, you'll see how valuable you are. You'll appreciate yourself more because you are a part of Him.

● **His body.** Physically, Jesus gave His body and blood to pay for your sin. You celebrate this every time you take communion. Now that Christ has risen, you can become part of His spiritual body (1 Corinthians 10:17). He is the Head of the body, and all Christians everywhere make up the other parts. Jesus depends on His body to accomplish His will, the way your head depends on your hands to open doors, or on your feet to pedal your bike. You're an important part of Jesus' body. If you're lazy or sin-sick, you affect other parts of the body.

● **His nature.** You also share Jesus' divine nature. You share in the "very being of God" (2 Peter 1:4, NEB), because His Spirit lives in you.

You can share more and more in this divine nature as you learn about God's promises and depend on them. Then He'll be able to work through you.

Do you want more and more of God's kindness and peace? Then learn to know Him better and better. For as you know Him better, He will give you, through His great power, everything you need for living a truly good life: He even shares His own glory and His own goodness with us! And by that same mighty power He has given us all the other rich and wonderful blessings He promised; for instance, the promise to save us from the lust and rottenness all around us, and to give us His own character (2 Peter 1:2-4, LB).

In the rest of 2 Peter 1 you'll find some excellent instructions about working out God's nature in you. See verses 5-11.

● **His calling and His honor.** A person's calling is his profession or vocation. Larry's calling is to be a physician, to heal the hurt bodies and spirits of patients who need him. As his wife, I share his calling. I help him care for people. I'm as committed to his work as he is. Because of that, I share in the esteem people have for him. I'm honored when he's honored.

Jesus' calling is to make peace between God and people. He wants to share this awesome task with you.

Therefore, dear brothers whom God has set apart for Himself—you who are chosen for heaven—I want you to think now about this Jesus who is God's Messenger and the High Priest of our faith (Hebrews 3:1, LB).

After Jesus returned to heaven, God passed on to you and me the ministry of peacemaking that Jesus began. (See 2 Corinthians 5:18.)

When Jesus was faced with dying a painful death, He knew that He had to suffer and die to pay for man's sin (John 12:7). But He also knew that God would honor Him because He was willing to do it. The Father promises to honor you also, if you are willing to share in Jesus' calling (John 12:26).

Paul said, "I beg you . . . to live and act in a way worthy of those who have been chosen for such wonderful blessings as these" (Ephesians 4:1, LB). Your life should reflect the humility, patience, strength, and love of Jesus, so that you can accomplish His mission for you.

This means that your *Number 1 priority* is to make Jesus known, by living like Him and by speaking His message, even when it costs you.

● **His glory.** Jesus told the Father, "I have given them the glory You gave Me." Do you know what that *glory* is? Something you may not expect:

> The glorious unity of being One, as We are—I in them and You in Me, all being perfected into One—so that the world will know You sent Me and will understand that You love them as much as You love Me (John 17:22-23, LB).

Because Jesus lives in you, you are united to the Father, *and to all other Christians.* Your goal should be to love other people in a way that makes the world see God in you.

● **His grace and favor.** God has given His grace and favor to you by accepting you. He promises that you'll always be able to come to Him. He wants to complete what He has begun in you. "God who began the good work within you will keep right on helping you grow in His grace until His task within you is finally finished on that day when Jesus Christ returns" (Philippians 1:6, LB).

To grow in God's grace means that you share in His goodness. You become more like Him.

● **His power.** Jesus has authority over all things, and the power to grant salvation to those who believe in Him. And just as He has power over evil, so do you, as His follower.

> In solemn truth I tell you, anyone believing in Me shall do the same miracles I have done, and even greater ones, because I am going to be with the Father. You can ask Him for *anything*, using My name, and I will do it, for this will bring praise to the Father because of what I, the Son, will do for you. Yes, ask *anything*, using My name, and I will do it! (John 14:12-14, LB)

Confidence! Confidence! Confidence!

Because Jesus has shared all these things with you, you can have endless confidence in what you have to share with the world. Jesus shared your suffering so that you can share His joy. You can experience that joy for yourself and pass it on to your world. When you use the nature, the grace, the favor, the honor, and the power He has given you, you'll become a mature person. God promises to give you the wisdom you need to do that!

> If . . . any of you does not know how to meet any particular problem he has only to ask God—who

gives generously to all men without making them feel foolish or guilty—and he may be quite sure that the necessary wisdom will be given him (James 1:5, PH).

The View from Down Here

1. Why was Jesus willing to share the negative aspects of human life for your sake?

2. How can you show Him you appreciate what He has done for you?

3. List the divine gifts Jesus has shared with you. Write down one experience for each of these from your everyday life to show how you use these gifts—or could use them.

4. When you don't know how to handle a situation, what should you do? (James 1:5) Why?

12

How to Get Close to God

God made you with a deep need for closeness. You want to snuggle, to touch, to be close. You want someone to love you for who you are. This need is so important that some babies who are denied closeness die. Even if they're well-fed, warmly clothed, and kept clean, they may die if they lack someone's touch and close personal involvement.

It's no accident that you sometimes need closeness; God made you with that desire. The sad thing is that in today's world, many people have forgotten the beauty and importance of close relationships. Families have lost much of the natural affection and closeness they should have. People tend to focus all their thoughts about intimacy and their need for it on just the sexual relationship, so close friendships are sometimes avoided.

Many teenagers (and adults) get involved in sexual

activity because they're hungry to be close to someone, to feel someone's touch, to be cared about. On the surface, sexual activity seems to offer this closeness. But when there's no spiritual and emotional intimacy on which to base the physical, the experience is disappointing.

God doesn't want you to throw away His gift of sex. He wants you to be pure, and to save sex for marriage. Even if you never marry, you can stay pure to honor God, and *He* can meet your need for nearness through friends and His own fellowship with you.

> You cannot say that our physical body was made for sexual promiscuity; it was made for God, and God is the answer to our deepest longings (1 Corinthians 6:13, PH).

You Are the Object of God's Love

God made you with a need for warm friendships because He wanted you to experience deep, close relationships with Him and with other people. He made all things for Himself—and that includes you. Did you know that He's preparing a special place for you to share with Him someday? (John 14:2-3) He wants you to be with Him forever. One of the most touching passages in all of Scripture is Jesus' prayer for His friends: "Father, I want them with Me—these You've given Me" (John 17:24, LB).

Look at the loving promise God gives to Israel, His chosen people:

> "Cheer up, don't be afraid. For the Lord your God has arrived to live among you. He is a mighty Saviour. He will give you victory. He will rejoice

over you in great gladness; He will love you and not accuse you." Is that a joyous choir I hear? No, it is the Lord Himself exulting over you in happy song (Zephaniah 3:16-17, LB).

In this same way, God delights in you. He wants you to have joy and fellowship with Him. His plans for you include hope and peace. (See Jeremiah 29:11.)

Mother Love and Lover Love

Various writers in the Old Testament refer many times to the tenderness and beauty of God's love for His children. "I have loved you with an everlasting love; therefore I have drawn you with lovingkindness" (Jeremiah 31:3, NASB). David could say of God, "He rescued me, because He delighted in me" (Psalm 18:19b, NASB).

Sometimes closeness to God is described in the context of our being His children. You might say He nourishes us and cuddles us, or sits us playfully on His knee. He talks to us tenderly, as a mother: "You will cry, and He will say, 'Here I am'" (Isaiah 58:9, NASB).

This tender way in which God cares for us reminds me of when my children were little. Returning from school, they would burst through the door in search of me.

"Mommy, where are you?" they'd ask. If I didn't answer quickly, I could hear panic in their voices. "Mommy, where *are* you?"

"Here I am," I would answer, and all the fear and confusion in their voices would disappear. My presence reassured them that all was well. God reassures us with His tender voice too.

Sometimes our closeness to God is described as the love of lovers. The Prophet Isaiah says to Israel:

> You will be called, "My delight is in her," and your land, "Married"; for the Lord delights in you, and to Him your land will be married. For as a young man marries a virgin, so your sons will marry you; and as the bridegroom rejoices over the bride, so your God will rejoice over you (Isaiah 62:4-5, NASB).

Have you read the Bible's Song of Solomon? This is a beautiful love poem which many scholars believe represents the love which exists between God and His people. This love song celebrates the beauty of physical and emotional closeness, of married love. I hope that you will read it, keeping in mind that God loves *you* with that kind of love.

Family Intimacy

Because no single comparison is adequate to describe the beauty and nearness of your relationship with God, the Bible uses many analogies. Your love is compared to other relationships besides that of a mother and child and that of lovers.

You are Jesus' brother. God has welcomed you into His inner family circle (Galatians 4:6-7). He wants you surrounded with His love. "Consider the incredible love that the Father has shown us in allowing us to be called 'children of God'—and that is not just what we are called, but what we *are*" (1 John 3:1, PH).

If you don't experience the love of your human family, it's especially important for you to understand that God loves you as His child. If it's true that a person can only learn to love by being loved, as many psychologists say, experiencing God's love can change your life. When you know His love, you'll be able to love others, even if your parents have failed you. I love the Psalmist David's prayer about this:

Don't forsake me, O God of my salvation. For if my father and mother should abandon me, You would welcome and comfort me (Psalm 27:9-10, LB).

If you've been abandoned, Jesus will give you welcome and comfort. He can heal your heart.

That's Some Love!

Do you know why *Romeo and Juliet* has become such a classic romantic story? It's because that young couple gave up everything—even their lives— because of their love for each other. We admire and idealize such wholehearted love.

Have you thought about how God's love for you is wholehearted? Jesus gave His life for you! And He promises that if you seek Him wholeheartedly you'll find Him (Jeremiah 29:13).

God wants this kind of devotion from you. He wants you to know Him better and better. He wants your love for Him to be the closest relationship in your life.

How to Be Intimate

You get close to God in the ways that you get to know people. The best way to begin is by spending a special time each day with God, as well as by sharing all your life with Him. God wants to be part of all you do; He doesn't want to be left out of your life in any way. The more you include Him, the better you get to know Him and the more you share together.

You get close to God by talking with Him, and by listening to what He has to say to you. You do this by praying, meditating, and by reading His Word. He has revealed Himself to you in the Bible. You can read it with the same enthusiasm and pleasure that you have when you read the letters you get from your boyfriend or girlfriend.

Real closeness depends on honesty and openness. Since God knows you better than anyone else can, you can be completely open with Him. He then has the freedom to help you change those feelings and thoughts that need changing.

Adam and Eve shattered their close friendship with God when they sinned. When you sin, the best thing you can do is to tell God about it immediately and ask Him to forgive you. If you don't confess your sin, He knows it anyway, and you feel awkward— just as you feel when you let down someone who has trusted you. Asking forgiveness clears the air between you.

Jewels and Journals

When you put God first in your life, He promises to reward you in many ways. He says He'll make good things happen to you. "Happy are all who search for God, and always do His will" (Psalm 119:2, LB).

Can you imagine God keeping a diary or a journal and making notes about you in it every day of your life?

Then those who feared and loved the Lord spoke often of Him to each other. And He had a Book of Remembrance drawn up in which He recorded the names of those who feared Him and loved to think about Him.

"They shall be Mine," says the Lord of Hosts, "in that day when I make up My jewels. And I will spare them as a man spares an obedient and dutiful son" (Malachi 3:17, LB).

Secure Enough to Risk

Have you ever been in love with someone? Or do you have a friend who's so close that he understands and accepts you completely? I have—and it gives me courage and confidence. I feel secure in that love, so I can afford to take risks in loving other people.

God's love is like that. Because He loves me, it doesn't matter so much whether people do or not. I'm not afraid of having people reject me (since I'm not desperate for their love or approval), so I can be more friendly and more open. I can love them without worrying whether they'll love me back. Because I'm more relaxed and more sincere, I end up having more friends.

When you're secure in God's love for you and give top priority to loving Him, you'll feel this kind of courage too. You'll feel so confident that you can take the risk of loving others. And if they do reject you, you'll be secure enough to take it. But you'll probably have more friends, because people need the love and friendship you offer them.

The View from Down Here

1. How does God meet your need for closeness?

2. Since God made you to be His friend and lover, how does He want you to take care of yourself?

3. Think about the ways your mother loves you. In what ways is God's love the same? In what ways is it different?

4. Think about your closest friend. How does that love make you feel? How does it compare with God's love for you?

5. Have you ever hurt someone you love? How did it make you feel? Do you ever hurt God's feelings? If so, do you apologize?

6. What will God do for you when you love Him wholeheartedly?

13

You Are Gift-Wrapped!

"Men need to give because they need to give themselves, and all their gifts are signs of that deep-seated and universal desire to give oneself. To live is to commit oneself."

Paul Tournier, *Gifts*

O. Henry, in his "Gift of the Magi," tells a beautiful story about gift-giving. Jim, a young husband, loves his wife Della deeply. She has long, golden hair, and the best gift he can think of to give her is a comb. He has only one treasure: a gold watch. Before Christmas he decides to sell his watch to buy a beautiful comb. Meanwhile, Della, who has nothing valuable except her lovely long hair, wants to buy a chain for his watch to show her love for him. She decides to sacrifice her hair in order to get the money to buy the watch chain. On Christmas morning they present their gifts—and discover in a moving way how precious their love for one another is.

The gifts which I treasure most are those that someone made or chose just for me. I like to save poems and notes—gifts of words my friends have written for me. And my engagement ring reminds me specially of Larry's love. He loved me enough to sell his own blood to the blood bank so he could buy the ring for me as a symbol of his love. That helps make it precious to me.

Different things are valuable to different people. In some parts of the world, for instance, salt is so scarce, yet so important to life, that people use it as a means of exchange. In other places, people use shells, or nuts, or stones. Many tribes in Peru use *achiote*, a paste made from red or black seeds, for money or gifts. It's valuable to them as a cosmetic, to keep away insects, and to use in rituals. But it seems that the most valuable gift anyone can ever give—in any culture—is oneself or one's child.

In the book *Peace Child*, Don Richardson tells the incredible story of two warring, cannibalistic groups in New Guinea who could only make peace with each other by giving a child away. One leader gave his son to the leader of the other group as a peace pact. This represented both risk and trust—as long as the child lived, the tribes would keep peace between them. The tribe with the boy would work hard to protect the child and rear him properly so that the other tribe would have no reason for revenge.

You—the Father's Gift to Jesus

People are the most expensive gifts ever bought or given in the whole universe! God paid the highest price anyone has ever paid in order to buy you back from sin. He paid for you by giving His Son, Jesus, to die for you. He figured that you were worth it.

Since God bought you at such a high price, can you guess what gift He chose to give Jesus? Jesus tells us that His disciples and others who believe in Him were given to Him by the Father (John 17:6, 9, 11). Isn't that incredible? The Father pays the highest price anyone could pay—His own Son—to buy *you* as a gift. Then He brings His Son back to life, and presents Him with the priceless gift which He bought through Christ's death—you and other people! Yes, you are God's gift to Jesus, if you believe in Jesus through the words of those men who were led to write God's Word for you (v. 20).

You—Jesus' Gift to the Father

At the end of time, when Jesus wants to give a gift to show His love for the Father, guess what He'll choose to give? Yes, you again! Because His people are His most precious possessions, Jesus will give us back to His Father, along with everything else that He has (1 Corinthians 15:28).

Jesus promises to give you a white robe, which represents His righteousness, when you are presented to the Father at the end of time. (See Revelation 7:9; 19:8.) This will be a spotless robe of fine linen. It will reflect Jesus' purity and perfection. When the Father looks at you then, He'll see Jesus' sinlessness.

I like to think of the robe Jesus will give me as His gift-wrapping. Because He loves me and wants to give me to the Father in the most beautiful way, He will wrap me in His own perfection to present me. The Father will look at me and see all of Jesus' beauty because I'll wear His robe. And that's how it will be for *you* too, if you belong to Him. You'll be spotless, without a wrinkle. You'll be holy. No one will blame you for any sin. You will be clothed in the brightness and glory of Jesus Himself! (See Colossians 1:22; Jude 24-25.)

The View from Down Here

1. What is the best gift that was ever given to you?

2. How does it compare with God's gift to you?

3. What is the most valuable gift you've ever given to someone else? What did your gift represent? What did it cost you?

4. What are you doing with God's greatest gift to you?

5. How are you storing up treasures for yourself in heaven?

6. How will Jesus "gift-wrap" you when He presents you to the Father?

14

Be a Becomer

My friend Laurie is wise and full of fun. She's bubbly and enthusiastic. Laurie trains teachers in post-graduate seminars and on-the-job-training courses. She can hardly believe she gets *paid* for doing what she loves to do! Her students love her because she's so full of life and so successful at integrating her Christian faith with her work. She firmly believes in helping people learn to use all their abilities and potential.

Laurie is what I call a *becomer*. She's a beautiful example of someone on the grow. To her, life is exciting and bursting with opportunities.

How did Laurie get to be what she is? She grew up in a Christian home and tried to do what was right. But that's not the whole secret.

"My parents weren't perfect," she says, "but I never felt the need to rebel. I wanted to please God."

Laurie grew up believing she had something to give to her world. She believed in her potential as God's child. She saw that her intelligence and love and dedication could change people's lives. After college she taught elementary school for four years. Then she had the opportunity to go to graduate school. With her husband's encouragement, she took advantage of her chance to contribute to education at a higher level. Now she's on the staff of a Christian college. Besides teaching there, she works with a public school system, training and evaluating teachers. She influences about 500 teachers a year with her strong and appealing Christian perspective. She even got to travel to South America last summer to teach missionary teachers from many countries. Laurie's changing her world—and yours too—by being nearly 100 percent of what God has called her to be. She's in love with God and uses the gifts He's given her.

You're Not Stuck

You can be a becomer too. Because of who you are to God, you don't have to be a prisoner of your past. You don't have to be stuck with sin, guilt, or fear. You can have victory over sin because Jesus took away its power in your life. No matter how badly you fail, you can always make a new start. That's freedom! That's relief!

You don't have to live with guilt that drags you down and keeps you feeling rotten about yourself. You don't have to carry that load; Jesus took it away from you. He took your sin and guilt as far away as the east is from the west. Now you can use your mental energy to grow instead of to push down your guilt.

You're free from fear too when you're a becomer. Did you know that fear is the worst inhibitor of creativity and growth? But through God you can overcome it. "For God has not given us a spirit of timidity, but of power and love and discipline (2 Timothy 1:7, NASB). Because you don't have to be afraid of God or of people, you can use your energy to grow, instead of fighting fear.

If you're in Christ you're a new person (2 Corinthians 5:17). Once you begin trusting in Jesus, you begin to grow. Just as you don't arrive in the world fully grown, so you don't start your Christian life as a mature believer. Spiritual growth takes time. The thing that's fantastic, though, is that *God* is building you, if you're letting Him. He doesn't leave you to yourself any more than your mom and dad let you raise yourself. Paul told the Philippian Christians, "He who began a good work in you will perfect it until the day of Christ Jesus" (Philippians 1:6, NASB). "For it is God who is at work within you, giving you the will and the power to achieve His purpose" (Philippians 2:13, PH).

Yes, God is involved in helping you grow. He gives you the *will* or desire, and also the *power* to grow. He doesn't leave you floundering on your own.

When you're a new person in Christ, you have unbelievable potential. You have two new resources which non-Christians lack. You have the Spirit of God—the Holy Spirit—living in you and you have God's Word, His revelation to man.

Doesn't it make sense that when you have God's own Spirit in you, you can be someone far better than ordinary? God will give you power and wisdom when you let Him control you.

You don't have to be in the dark about what God wants or expects from you. He tells you clearly in His Word. That saves you from the kind of doubt and confusion that your non-Christian friends have to struggle with. God's Word gives you a master plan, the safety limits, and the principles for living your life successfully.

Know What You Have to Give

Because you are God's child and are entrusted with His message, you have something to give to your world. You don't have to flounder around looking for yourself, as so many young people do. You already know you have a place in the world, and an important role to fulfill. You can have the courage to give yourself away, as a means of making God known.

Instead of being a taker, you can be a giver. Instead of being a hurter, you can be a helper. Instead of adding to the woes of the world, you can dig in, sort out, and solve problems. You can have the confidence that the love and help you offer will positively change people and situations around you. You can create an environment around you which allows others to flourish, to discover who God made them to be.

Jesus could afford to give Himself away. He knew He was the Son of God, so He was not threatened by being a Servant. His self-esteem wasn't lowered because He touched lepers, washed fishermen's feet, and cooked breakfast on an open fire. He thought no less of Himself as God's Son because some people scoffed at Him and the Pharisees plotted to murder Him.

Paul tells us, "Have this attitude in yourselves, which was also in Christ Jesus" (Philippians 2:5, NASB). He humbled Himself, and was willing to die in order for someone else to receive life. You can be like that because of who you are to God.

What Are You Becoming?

God's plan is for you to become more like Jesus, the only perfect Person who ever lived. When God made you, He planned that you would become like Jesus (Romans 8:29). You're somewhat like your parents, or certain friends, because you associate with them. You become like Jesus by spending time with Him, by talking with Him and learning from Him, and by letting Him live in you.

My daughter Kathryn says she's never seen an ugly Christian. No matter what a person looks like, Jesus' love and Spirit shine out so that Christians look good to her. Being like Jesus can even make you look better!

How Do You Know When You've Arrived?

You won't be perfect, of course, until Jesus returns and takes you out of this world. But there are ways you can tell how far you've come—whether you are becoming like Jesus or not.

Look over this checklist and see how much you're revealing about God to the people around you:

☐ I'm sensitive to others' needs and I'm eager to tell them about God's love.

☐ I'm enthusiastic about sharing God's Word and helping others get to know Him.

☐ I openly love people and let them see God in my life.

☐ I have—and show—peace, joy, patience, kindness, generosity, truthfulness, and self-control in my life. (See Galatians 5:22-23.)

☐ My main goal is to honor God in every area of my life.

Future Unlimited

When you give back to God all the abilities, talents, and opportunities He has given you, you have a wide-open future ahead. My friend Laurie didn't know about all the neat opportunities God would bring to her. She followed Him wholeheartedly each step, and He has kept on bringing her chances to grow. If you follow Him, He will do that for you too.

God wants you to be the best in what you do so that you can influence the world for Him to your fullest potential. He wants you to have the kind of success that reflects Him—His love, His wisdom, His holiness!

Let me tell you about another becomer, Dr. Olive Shell. Olive is one of my favorite people, because she lets God live through her. She is 73, but believe me, she doesn't sit around knitting or wasting away. I recently spent two weeks with her, traveling by dugout canoe through the Amazon jungle of Peru. We were delivering just-printed copies of the New Testament in several Cashibo villages. Olive spent about 30 years living among the Cashibos and translating God's Word for them. She helped them in countless ways. She literally gave her life away to bring God's Good News to them. She could retire now, but she has chosen instead to go to Africa to start a new job as a literacy consultant.

During the years of her self-giving, God helped Olive do many things. She earned a master's degree and a doctorate in linguistics. She helped start a teacher training school and helped train hundreds of Indian teachers. She published many scholarly papers in linguistics and anthropology. She taught in leading universities. She survived two killer diseases. She is known and loved by thousands of people. Because of her faithful service and her discipline in translating God's Word, hundreds of people will go to heaven. And besides all that, Olive still has the energy to ride a motorcycle and trek jungle trails. She's slender, agile, energetic, and has a gorgeous tan any teenager would envy. She gave herself away—to God and the Cashibos—and look what He has given her in exchange!

Olive didn't know in the beginning that all of this would happen. She was faithful to God one step at a time, believing that He would bring what was best for her.

Just as your future on earth is wide open when you give yourself to God, so is your eternal future.

> But our homeland is in heaven, where our Saviour the Lord Jesus Christ is; and we are looking forward to His return from there. When He comes back He will take these dying bodies of ours and change them into glorious bodies like His own, using the same mighty power that He will use to conquer all else everywhere (Philippians 3:20-21, LB).

Yes, you'll have a new body—one worth lots more than $6 million. You'll be freed from the limitations of time and space. You will live forever!

So What's the Difference? This Is!

You now know your worth to God, so you can value yourself highly. You have the most lofty and exciting purpose anyone could have—to bring honor and glory to God by revealing Him to others! He wants you to reflect His divine nature for everyone to see. You're the world's light and salt!

Realizing your worth helps you go through both tough times and success. You can survive the most terrible experiences, just as Jesus did. You can endure any ridicule or humiliation, without being devasted or dehumanized. You can take it if people scoff at you or put you down, confident that God will use anything that happens to you to make you mature. (See Romans 8:28.)

But for many people, success is harder to handle than problems. When a person is successful, it's easy for him to forget God. He may see himself as a "self-made" man, a superior person. But if you recognize that *God* is the Source of all your ability and opportunity, you can continue to grow and become a mature person.

Knowing who you are to God also gives you tremendous confidence and zest. You can grab opportunities as they come. And you can risk giving yourself to people. As Jesus gave Himself to the blind, the lepers, and the poor, you can give your love to the lonely and hurting people you know.

Knowing God's purpose for you, you can be so stable and steady that you can resist negative, destructive pressures. And you can discover how great it feels to reflect God's love to others and show them that they're special to God too!